Visual Anthropology: Photography as a Research Method

John Collier, Jr.

STUDIES IN ANTHROPOLOGICAL METHOD

DATE DUE

S

SOUTHERN
OCT 1974
BOUND

STUDIES IN
ANTHROPOLOGICAL METHOD

General Editors

GEORGE AND LOUISE SPINDLER
Stanford University

VISUAL ANTHROPOLOGY:
PHOTOGRAPHY AS A RESEARCH METHOD

VISUAL ANTHROPOLOGY:
PHOTOGRAPHY AS
A RESEARCH METHOD

JOHN COLLIER, JR.

San Francisco State College

HOLT, RINEHART AND WINSTON

New York   Chicago   San Francisco   Atlanta

Dallas   Montreal   Toronto   London

INDIANA
PURDUE
LIBRARY
NOV 1974
FORT WAYNE

WITHDRAWN

Copyright © 1967 by Holt, Rinehart and Winston, Inc.

All rights reserved

Library of Congress Catalog Number: 67–22607

ISBN 0-03-065245-6

Printed in the United States of America

4567   059   9876543

All photographs by John Collier, Jr., and are repro-
duced (on the indicated pages) by courtesy of the
following:

The Farm Quarterly (pp. xxii and 55)

Dr. Allan R. Holmberg, Cornell-Peru Project at
Vicos (pp. 18, 63, 68, and 83)

Standard Oil Co., N.J. (pp. 26 and 78)

from John Collier, Jr. and Anibal Buitron, *The
Awakening Valley,* University of Chicago Press,
1949 (p. 31)

Dr. Alexander H. Leighton, Stirling County Study,
Cornell University (p. 34)

Dr. Bernard Siegel, Stanford University (pp. 8 and
115)

This writing is dedicated to

ALEXANDER H. LEIGHTON

for his persistence in mastering

the whole view,

and to

ROY E. STRYKER

for bountiful

photographic opportunity;

and for human integrity

in photography.

W E NO LONGER describe for the sake
of describing, from a caprice and
a pleasure of rhetoricians. We consider that man cannot be separated
from his surroundings, that he is
completed by his clothes, his house,
his city, and his country; and hence
we shall not note a single phenomenon
of his brain and heart without looking
for the causes or the consequence in
his surroundings . . . I should define
description: "An account of environment which determines and completes
man." . . . In a novel, in a study of
humanity, I blame all description which
is not according to that definition.

Emile Zola in *The Experimental Novel*

FOREWORD

ABOUT THE SERIES

Anthropology has been, since the turn of the century, a significant influence shaping Western thought. It has brought into proper perspective the position of our culture as one of many and has challenged universalistic and absolutistic assumptions and beliefs about the proper condition of man. Anthropology has been able to make this contribution mainly through its descriptive analyses of non-Western ways of life. Only in the last decades of its comparatively short existence as a science have anthropologists developed systematic theories about human behavior in its transcultural dimensions, and only very recently have anthropological techniques of data collection and analysis become explicit and in some instances replicable.

Teachers of anthropology have been handicapped by the lack of clear, authoritative statements of how anthropologists collect and analyze relevant data. The results of fieldwork are available in the ethnographies and they can be used to demonstrate cultural diversity and integration, social control, religious behavior, marriage customs, and the like, but clear, systematic statements about how the facts are gathered and interpreted are rare in the literature readily available to students. Without this information the alert reader of anthropological literature is left uninformed about the process of our science, knowing only of the results. This is an unsatisfying state of affairs for both the student and the instructor.

This series is designed to help solve this problem. Each study in the series focuses upon manageable dimensions of modern anthropological methodology. Each one demonstrates significant aspects of the processes of gathering, ordering, and interpreting data. Some are highly selected dimensions of methodology. Others are concerned with the whole range of experience involved in studying a total society. These studies are written by professional anthropologists who have done fieldwork and have made significant contributions to the science of man and his works. In them the authors explain how they go about this work, and to what end. We think they will be helpful to students who want to know what processes of inquiry and ordering stand behind the formal, published results of anthropology.

ABOUT THE AUTHOR

John Collier's qualifications are those of a fieldworker and an observer of culture. In his role as photographer he has brought special sensitivity to recognition and recording of the field circumstance.

Collier's first fieldwork was in the early forties with the Farm Security Administration photographic team led by Roy E. Stryker. Here, working with Edwin Rosskam, Arthur Rothstein, John Vachon, Jack Delano, and Russell Lee, Collier was educated in the social and economic content of the documentary visual record. When Stryker moved from government to industry, much of his staff moved with him, and Collier spent four roving years recording the role of petroleum as an agent of change, from the arctic to the tropics. This experience brought him to the challenge of cultural significance in photographic imagery.

In 1946 Collier collaborated with Anibal Buitron, Ecuadorean anthropologist, in an experimental study to record with the camera the complexity of culture and processes of change. *The Awakening Valley,* by Collier and Buitron, reported on this effort of combining photography and ethnography.

From this point Collier moved directly into anthropology. For three years he worked as a research assistant with Dr. Alexander H. Leighton, of Cornell University, exploring and testing out various photographic methodologies that could open the door to the nonverbal content of culture. These studies included cross-cultural fieldwork in the Maritimes of Canada and the Navajo Reservation. Next Collier worked for a year assembling for Dr. Allan R. Holmberg a photographic baseline of the culture of Vicos against which to evaluate change in the Peru-Cornell Project. A comprehensive photographic ethnography was prepared, which awaits publication.

For the past six years Collier has devoted his time to teaching. He has lectured at Stanford University and the University of California at Berkeley, and has taught photography for the California School of Fine Arts in San Francisco. He is now assistant professor in the Department of Anthropology and in the School of Education at San Francisco State College.

ABOUT THE BOOK

The dimensions brought together in this book by John Collier extend far beyond a technical manual on how to take good photographs. It is a statement of research procedure and a treatise on observation and interpretation. Though addressed to anthropologists it is relevant to all the behavioral sciences wherever the recording and interpretation of visual data are significant.

Most anthropologists take a camera with them into the field. Some take expensive equipment with definite plans to do extensive photography related to their research. Others take along a simple camera they use for other purposes at home, and bring it along pretty much as an afterthought. Most anthropologists take photographic equipment with them, but too often with no clear concept of what to do with the camera in the field or what to do with the pictures once they are taken.

Usually an anthropologist takes a photograph to illustrate a finding that he has already decided is significant, frequently with publication in mind. He waits until whatever it is happens, then points his camera at it. His camera then is incidental to his research activity and comes into use late in the fieldwork period. He uses the camera not as a research technique, but as a highly selective confirmation that certain things are so, or as a very selective sample of "reality." This is a legitimate use of the camera but falls far short of the potential of photography.

John Collier shows us how the camera can be used inductively, as all research techniques should be used in fieldwork. The fieldworker can take a picture of something he does not fully, or sometimes even partially understand, something that he can record for later understanding. And the explanation can come not only from his own accumulating insight but from a native informant as well. Most significantly the photograph can be used in interviewing to elicit responses that serve to unlock the real content of the photograph. No better way has as yet been devised to record a "slice of reality" that is almost infinitely complex, that is accurate and objective, and that has direct and explicable (under favorable conditions of elicitation) meaning to the informant. The photograph when explained by a "native" (anyone who is at home in the environment) becomes psychological reality.

The camera, as the author explains, has other uses for the anthropologist as well. Besides using the camera as an inductive technique, it may be used to standardize and objectivize research interpretation. Project workers may examine photographs of significant phenomena together (as in a field survey of housing as an index of poverty and affluence discussed in chapter 3) and settle problems of rating standardization that would take weeks of on-the-spot collaboration, or would otherwise go unsolved, to the serious detriment of the study.

The author makes it abundantly clear that the camera creates a role for the anthropologist who uses it. Rather than creating barriers between the fieldworker and his subjects the camera can help reduce barriers. The photographs become something the fieldworker can reward the informant with. More importantly, they can clarify for the native the project's research needs. The camera provides entree and creates a favorable and appropriate role niche for the student. There are pitfalls, of course, and the author helps the reader to anticipate them.

The camera then, as John Collier describes its use, has significant purposes beyond the recording and documentation of what is known to be significant. The professional anthropologist or student who reads this study will add a new dimension to his armamentarium of research and appraisal techniques. The student who studies it will be able to anticipate this new dimension and integrate it into his emerging professional character structure, to the benefit of his future research, teaching, and publication. The layman who reads it will acquire a new appreciation of what observation means, and of the rich visual texture of social life.

Most of the book is devoted to the research uses of the camera, and the philosophy and criteria guiding this research. One chapter covers the minimal technical knowledge required to employ photography effectively in the field. Considered from the novice's point of view, what could be a very technical and forbidding chapter turns out to be very clear and basically simple. A final chapter is devoted to the use of the movie camera in anthropology. Here the reader is given one of the most succinct yet richly meaningful introductions to the use of film in behavioral science and education that is available. It is made very clear that making a useful film requires much more than a movie camera and a large budget. Planning, foresight, at least minimal technical knowledge, and an intimate knowledge of the culture are essential. For these reasons the uses of the movie and still camera are quite different. The latter can be used inductively as a technique of entree, rapport-gaining, and inquiry, in the early stages of research, as well as a technique for recording visual data for future analysis. The movie camera must be used with foreknowledge, and usually after intimate knowledge of the culture has been acquired by other means. But the film itself may be used in the laboratory as visual data, and is incomparable as a record of the fluid and emotionally contextualized reality the fieldworker actually experiences.

GEORGE AND LOUISE SPINDLER
General Editors
Stanford, July 1967

PREFACE

It is through perception, largely visual and auditory, that we respond to the humanness that surrounds us. Our recognition of cultural phenomena is controlled by our ability to respond and to understand. The camera is an optical system—it has no selective process—and alone it offers no means of evading the need for perceptive sensitivity. Therefore, I begin this volume with a discussion of observation, go on to relate the visual content of photography to the theoretical framework of field research, and consider finally the technology of the photographer's craft in both still pictures and movies.

Some readers may want to reverse this process, preferring to introduce themselves first to technical photographic skills before facing the problem of carrying through a field study. This book has been designed to allow such an order of study. Other readers may find the technical chapters too schematic or even oversimplified. But with the limitation of length I feel both the humanistic and the theoretical problems of photographic observation are more important than a lengthy handbook on how-to-do-it photography. Through years of teaching photography to journalists, artists, and scientists, I have found it negative to allow technique to come between the photographer and the human circumstance of involvement, observational refinement, and selectivity. Rarely have I found a lack of technical skill to be a serious problem in any of these three fields of photography. Yet many times I have found the fascination of possessing a complex camera and the mystique of technical paraphernalia a critical block to making significant camera records.

Hence, in this writing I have chosen to present the drama of the field study and the involvement of research first, so there will be a genuine reason and motivation for making photographs and mastering a sufficient technique to carry to conclusion a project of photographic analysis.

JOHN COLLIER, JR.

San Francisco, Calif.
July 1967

ACKNOWLEDGMENTS

The roots of this book go back to the Farm Security Administration and the photographic foresight of Roy E. Stryker. The work's scientific significance begins with research in collaboration with Alexander H. Leighton and the staff of the Stirling County Study, particularly Robert N. Rapaport, Seymour Parker, William Magill, and Marc-Adélard Tremblay, and with the generous support of the Wenner-Gren Foundation and the Carnegie Corporation of New York. Further experiences I draw upon include work on the Fruitland Navajo Project with Tom T. Sasaki and William A. Ross, and a year with Allan R. Holmberg's Cornell-Peru Project in Vicos.

Earlier writing on this subject was made possible by a Fellowship from the John Simon Guggenheim Memorial Foundation and the encouragement of its director, Henry Moe. The material has been worked over many times in six years of teaching at San Francisco State College.

The present volume was written in editorial collaboration with Mary Trumbull Collier, who participated in many of the field studies cited, and who made the statistical analysis and charts for the photographic study of Indian relocation. The shape of the book is also a product of the critical reading of my friends John and Casey Adair, John and Patricia Hitchcock, Edward T. Hall, and the series editors, George and Louise Spindler.

I am indebted to many colleagues whose experiences in taking and using photographs have enriched my own. In particular I want to thank those who have generously given me permission to draw upon their experiences and insights as examples: John Adair, Paul Byers, Alyce Cathey, Bernard S. Cohn, George Collier, Paul Ekman, Byron Harvey, William Heick, Dwight Heath, John and Patricia Hitchcock, Alexander H. Leighton, Michael Mahar, Margaret Mead, Morris Opler, David Peri, Arthur Rotman, Bernard Siegel, George and Louise Spindler, and Robert Wharton.

Special thanks go to James Hirabayashi for permission to report on our part in his research on Indian Urban Integration; to Joanne Leonard who photographed one of the Indian families; and to the project fieldworkers with whom I worked directly, Luis Kemnitzer, Gordon Krutz, Richard Moore, Frank Norrick, and Daniel Swett.

CONTENTS

VISUAL ANTHROPOLOGY:
PHOTOGRAPHY AS A RESEARCH METHOD

Navajo weaver and spinner. The scope of the camera's eye covers more than the technicalities of the textile craft: age relationships, elements of acculturation, inventory of property, use of space. Can the human eye, unaided, recall this complex whole?

1

The Challenge of Observation
and the Nature of Photography

THIS BOOK IS in general about human interaction and observation. In particular, it explores the goal of whole vision in anthropology approached through the use of photography. For many reasons, we moderns are not good observers, and I feel here the sharp focus of the camera might help us to see more, and accurately. The camera is not presented as a cure-all for our visual limitations, but as an extension of our perception. Only human response can open the camera's eye meaningfully for anthropology. Therefore, in order to grasp the function of the camera in research we must first turn our attention to the phenomena of human observation.

There are problems in modern perception that must be recognized if we are going to make reliable observations of culture. Learning to observe visually, to see culture in all of its complex detail, can be a challenge to the fieldworker. The fragmented nature of modern life makes it difficult to respond to the whole view. The observer's capacity for rounded vision is certainly related to the degree of his involvement with his environment. We moderns have drifted out of an embracing relationship with our surroundings, for we usually deal only with parts of this comprehensive scheme.

In contrast, the perception of the aborigine is related to his interaction with his total environment. The native with limited technology necessarily has to live in harmony with surrounding nature. He has to be an astute observer of all his world or perish! Natural forces surround him and he is constantly struggling to survive among them. When the Eskimo leaves his hut to go sealing, he must deal firsthand with every element of his surroundings and be master of every available technique to cope with it. Often he must make each life and death decision independently. These decisions determine whether he finds game or not, whether he makes it home through the icefloes or is swept away on the Arctic seas.

Our cultural development, on the other hand, has been oriented to commanding nature by supertechnology carried on collectively by the superorganization of fragmented functions. We believe we are masters of our world and no longer have to deal constantly or personally with natural forces. This security has limited the range of phenomena that we as individuals have to observe in order to survive, and we in turn have become limited observers when compared to the aboriginal hunter.

Only at a few points in our daily lives do we have to make survival decisions entirely by our own senses. We jam on the brakes when we see a red light, accelerate when the light goes green. Or we step unwarily out across the pedestrian lanes, confident that other specialists will guide their movements by the same signals.

It is true that within select areas we too are keen visual analysts. In our own highly educated fields we see with more precision than any aborigine, though when we leave these areas we may be visually illiterate. The radiologist can diagnose tuberculosis from a lung shadow on an x-ray; the bacteriologist can recognize bacilli in his microscope. Yet when these technicians leave their laboratories they can find their way home efficiently with only a glance at their surroundings, or up to the heavens to see whether they will be caught in the rain. Their raincoats are left behind for the radio report said, "Fair tonight and Tuesday with gentle westerly winds." Other specialists made highly technical instrumental observations to reach these conclusions for them. It is only by considering the sum of all of our specialized visions that we can consider ourselves the most acute observers in man's history.

Unquestionably the personal blindness that obscures our individual viewing is related to the detachment that is possible in our urban mechanized society. We learn to see only what we pragmatically need to see. We go through our days with blinders, dealing with and observing only a fraction of our surroundings. And when we do see critically it is often with the aid of some technology.

But many shrewd observations are made with instruments. We can observe life in a drop of water with our microscopes, look out into celestial space with telescopes, and even see back in history with instrumental reading of carbon 14. We observe with slide rules, computers, light meters, and radarscopes; these instruments have still further specialized our vision. Instrumental vision has allowed us to see elements very near and very far; in great abstraction of light, sound, heat and cold; in measures of pressure and of stress.

The camera is another instrumental extension of our senses but one that is highly unspecialized and can record on the lowest possible scale of abstraction. The camera by its optical character has whole vision. No matter how select a unit we might wish to photograph, the camera instrument faithfully records this specialized part, and then all the other associated parts within focus and scope of its lens. This capacity should make the camera a most valuable tool for the observer.

The adaptability of camera vision has made photography a standard of accurate perception in many fields. Many disciplines depend upon the camera eye to see selectively what the human eye cannot, whether this be to trace the development of plant fungi, to look for soft landings on the moon, or more popularly to decide the photo finish of the Kentucky Derby.

The Image with a Memory

The camera's aid to observation is not new; Leonardo da Vinci described its principles. Light entering a tiny hole of a wall of a darkened room forms on the opposite wall an inverted image of whatever was outside. The *camera obscura,* or literally the darkened room, was the first camera where artists could study projected reality, the character of light, the delineation of perspective. By the eighteenth century cameras had shrunk from a room large enough to hold a man to a portable 2-foot box with the peephole replaced by a ground lens. Tracing paper was used instead of film, and exact copies of reality were traced right side up on a ground glass that resembled closely the mirrored image of the modern Graflex camera.

The *camera obscura* could retain the projected image only by a manual tracing, a laborious and often stilted operation. In 1837 Louis Daguerre perfected the first efficient light sensitive plate, the mirror with a memory. The daguerreotype introduced photography to the world. This relatively cheap, rapid, mobile imagery changed the character of photographic rendering. Now it was not only perspective and principles of light that were recorded for study, but the human image, a precise memory of exactly how a particular person looked, that could be examined again and again by any number of observers, now or years later. The camera image because of this facility ushered in a new phase of human understanding that continues to expand our social thinking.

The persistent problem in centuries past and in our human relations now is to see the other fellow as he really is. Before the invention of photography, the concept of world humanity, flora, and fauna was often a fantastic one. This is why the camera with its impartial vision has been, since its inception, a clarifier and a modifier of ecological and human understanding. Man has always used images to give form to his concepts of reality. It was the artists' imagery that defined heaven and hell, the shape of evil, demons, threatening savages—the images of people who were so startlingly different. People thought by means of these representations which generally bore out what the artists wanted to see or were shocked by seeing.

The excitement that greeted the invention of photography was the sense that man for the first time could see the world as it *really* was. This confidence was born from a recognition that photography was an optical process, not an art process. Its images were made by real light, as natural as a shadow cast by a hand, rubbings taken from stones, or animal tracks on the trail. Critics can justly point out that this acceptance of the camera's convincing realism is at times more of a mystique than a reality. Yet for multitudes, the photographic record is true because "the camera cannot lie." This simplification is, of course, supported only by the camera's accurate recording of certain physical aspects of reality such as views of the pyramids and Niagara Falls. But despite any discrepancies between reality and the touted realism of the camera's vision, photography has greatly affected modern thinking. Men have changed their views of the world to approximate the universal view of the camera.

Photo-journalists' views are certainly edited ones. The worthwhile element of these records is that because of the impartial process of the camera's vision, even these edited documents contain a sufficient number of nonverbal truths to allow the audience to reconstruct schematic reality and to form concepts supported by what they recognize as valid evidence. Photo-reportage projects have changed social thinking dramatically, and demonstrated the fact-presenting value of the camera. The documentary records of Mathew Brady, commissioned by Abraham Lincoln, were among the first impartial views of war. These were not hasty snapshots, but time exposure records of the fallen bodies, the burnt wreckage of buildings, and the faces of the maimed and the captured. Gone were the brave banners and charging horses; Brady recorded the effects of war, not simply its dramatic actions. Several decades later police reporter Jacob Riis turned to the camera to present slum conditions in New York City. Unwieldy view cameras and powder flash recorded such scenes as the "Bandits' Roost," interiors of slum homes and schools. These early records of urban anthropology helped establish the first building codes and apartment regulations. In the first decades of this century, the sociologist Lewis Hine recorded the entry of immigrants through Ellis Island, preserving the original look of the European before he "melted" into American life. Hine also turned his camera on child labor and his images were influential in passing the first child labor laws (Newhall 1949:167–173). Observation, synthesis, and action—is that not the essence of applied anthropology?

Paralleling these urban studies was the work of Edward S. Curtis, photographer and amateur descriptive ethnologist, who carried out extensive photographic salvage studies of American Indian culture, recording native life from the Arctic to the Southwest. Certainly they are history, but they are also our only visual record of many Indian cultural patterns that now have perished, a "salvage" effort comparable in spirit to that of the late Dr. Samuel A. Barrett.

The effect of photography as an aspect of reality is felt throughout modern life. In a sense we think photographically and certainly communicate photographically. The nonverbal language of photorealism is the language that is most understood interculturally and cross-culturally. This fluency of recognition is the basic reason the camera can be of such importance in anthropological communication and analysis.

The Camera as a Research Tool

What are the camera's special assets, that make photography of great value to anthropology? The camera is an automative tool, but one that is highly sensitive to the attitudes of its operator. Like the tape recorder it documents mechanically, but does not by its mechanics necessarily limit the sensitivity of the human observer —it is a tool of extreme selectivity.

The camera's machinery allows us to see without fatigue; the last exposure is just as detailed as the first. The memory of film replaces the notebook and insures complete notation under the most trying circumstance. The reliably repetitive operation of the camera allows for comparable observations of an event as many times as the needs of research demand. This mechanical support of field observation extends the possibilities of critical analysis, for the camera record contributes a control factor to visual observation. Not only is it a check on eye memory, but further, it allows for an absolute check of position and identification in a congested and changing cultural event.

Photography is a legitimate abstracting process in observation. It is one of the first steps in evidence refinement that turns raw circumstances into data that is manageable in research analysis. Photographs are precise records of material reality. They are also documents that can be filed and cross-filed as can verbal statements. Photographic evidence can be endlessly duplicated, enlarged or reduced in visual dimension, and fitted into many schemes of diagrams, and by scientific reading, into many statistical designs.

A large volume of photographic content is tangible. Any number of analysts can read the same elements in exactly the same manner. To be sure this takes training, but so does the reading of maps and bacteriological slides.

But what are the camera's limitations? They are fundamentally the limitations of the men who use them. Again we face the problem of whole and accurate human observation. No field is more aware of this challenge than anthropology. Seeing the stranger as he "really" is, in ethnography as in all human relations, too often becomes a casualty of our personal values. Social scientists appreciate that there is little we can see that is truly free from bias or personal projection. The realism of this anxiety of course extends to photographic vision as well as to eye vision.

Ethnographers have with considerable enthusiasm accepted photography as the clearest illustration of culture. Yet there has been little research in anthropology actually based upon photography. Not unreasonably, anthropologists have not particularly trusted the mechanics of the camera to defeat impressionism and the value manipulation of vision. Only the physical anthropologists with their body measurements, and the archeologists with their potsherds, burials, and post holes, confidently count on the camera to make research records.

High points on the trail of direct research accomplished with the camera are quickly recounted. Pioneer photographer Eadweard Muybridge, seeking a method to catch elusive action the eye could not follow, perfected an early method of time and motion studies. In 1887 he published *Animal Locomotion,* eleven volumes with 20,000 photographs of every imaginable motion of animals and men, including a mother spanking a child. While Muybridge's effort was conceived as a service to artists seeking realism in their drawings, his method was seized upon by a French physiologist, Marey, to study minutely the movement of animals, birds, and even insects. In the process Marey developed a camera with a moving plate with which he could photograph twelve frames per second, the forerunner of the movie camera. Marey's frame-by-frame analysis provided a method of investigation which has been pushed into every corner of the life sciences, in combination with microscope and x-ray (Michaelis 1955:118; and Newhall 1949).

In the less controllable field of human behavior, probably the most intensive work with photography is that of Arnold Gesell, director for many years of the Yale Clinic of Child Development. Based on the photographic record of many children day-by-day and at scheduled intervals over many years, Gesell drew up a timetable or sequence of the normal maturation and social development process. This sequence has profoundly influenced child psychology not only as a science but as it is practiced by the parents of the children in our culture (1934, 1945).

Gregory Bateson and Margaret Mead made the first, and as yet unparalleled, saturated photographic research in another culture, the results of which were published in *Balinese Character* (1942). Since this work, both have continued to use photography, Mead in her continuing concern with child development (for example, Mead and Macgregor 1951), and Bateson particularly in the study of nonverbal communication (1963; and Ruesch and Kees 1956).

The field of ethnographic photography is still one of the most specialized and experimental. Edward T. Hall referred to photographic data continually in the development of his concepts of nonverbal communication (see *The Silent Language,* 1959), and he studied photographs to stabilize many aspects of the significance of the use of space, or "proxemics" (see *The Hidden Dimension,* 1966). Hall always has a camera with him to make notes of interaction and communication wherever he encounters such phenomena. At present he is identifying peaks of communication by means of photography. Ray L. Birdwhistell used photography to systematize the study of culturally patterned posture and gesture, which he terms "kinesics" (1952), a field virtually impossible to approach without photography. Paul Byers, combining the skills of a professional photographer with anthropological training, is working toward a clearer understanding of photography as a three-way process of communication involving photographer, subject, and viewer, each in an active and expandable role (Mead 1963:178–179). Oswald Werner, now at Northwestern University, also brought the skills of professional photography to anthropology. His thesis surveyed the field of practices and potentials of ethnographic photography; an abstract of this work was distributed (1961), but the complete paper is as yet unpublished.

Nevertheless, in the field of anthropology as a whole, photography remains an extraordinary rather than a usual method. No work comparable to *Balinese Character* has been published since it appeared in 1942, and there are only occasional references to the use of the camera in anthropological literature.

It seems to me, the basic visual inhibitions of anthropology have discouraged the use of photography as a research tool. One anthropologist expressed to me his frustrations about photographs: "It's not that photographs are not good. They're too good. Photographs are just more raw realism. They contain everything. We have worked out techniques for digesting verbal data, but what can we do with photographs?" Indeed this is the challenge. One photograph can contain a thousand references. And even more confounding, most photographs are a minute time sample—a hundredth of a second slice of reality. Until fieldworkers know what to photograph, when and how many times to photograph—and why—anthropologists will see no functional way to use the camera. Finally, if researchers are without reliable keys to photographic content, if they do not know what is positive responsible evidence and what is intangible and strictly impressionistic, anthropology will not be able to use photographs as data, and there will be no way of moving from raw imagery to the synthesized statement.

This volume will attempt to outline how the camera can be used to explore and to analyse, so that we can use photography not only to *show* what we have already found out by some other means, but actually to extend our visual processes and to help us *find out more* about the nature of man and his multi-faceted cultures.

2

Orientation and Rapport

PHOTOGRAPHY'S PRACTICAL PLACE in fieldwork can be demonstrated by relating its functions to the development of the field study. The introductory step in many projects is an ethnographic overview or a phase of descriptive study. This period is necessarily one of orientation and education of the researchers. It is a phase of fact gathering about the total environment under study, often essential to obtaining a wide view within which cultural detail can find an organic place. A grasp of ecology and cultural geography opens an orderly road to future levels of investigation.

As research progresses the general view is necessarily laid aside in efforts to make a more penetrating study of selected aspects. Fieldwork reasonably narrows its focus in search of *particular* evidence pertinent to the goals of the research. The reconnaissance of the initial ethnography interrelates, guides, and gives setting to this cultural trenching and sampling. As understanding deepens, research methods become increasingly specialized, interviewing more structured, speculations more analytical with the support of psychological examinations, tests, and questionnaires. In this period specialists from many disciplines may enter the field, each viewing the people and their culture differently, contributing additional understanding to the research. With this multiplicity, the background of the whole view as one basis of homogeneous understanding is more important than ever.

In the third and final operation the study comes to the synthesis phase where the research must be developed into conclusions. In this phase photographic evidence must, of course, be abstracted in the same way as all other data, verbalized, translated into statistics, even computed electronically in order to become a genuine part of the fabric of scientific statement. If this process does not take place the camera is not a source of research in modern anthropology. This book will follow the course of these three phases, referring again and again to actual and to hypothetical research situations for examples of the various processes.

In line with the culture of anthropology, which places considerable value on intensive firsthand experiences, it is in the initial phase of field research that photography has had its most enthusiastic use. This appreciation is realistic, as the fore-

A long view of a Spanish-American community in New Mexico, showing its setting within the ecology. There is an ample wood supply in the surrounding hills, pasture and grazing lands on the upper mesa, and subsistence irrigated farming in the valley lands.

most characteristic of the camera is its ability to record material that the camera operator himself cannot recognize or yet understand. Photography offers the stranger in the field a means of recording large areas authentically, rapidly and with great detail, and a means of storing away complex descriptions for future analysis.

Sweeping photographs can set the stage for research. Long views establish relationships of ecology and community. They hold in place the broad view within which many levels and disciplines of abstraction can take place.

When we use photography as a method and a source of orientation, we make use of its popular illustrative function. More important, we exploit photographs as independent specimens of data, not fully perceived until held in place by the camera record. It is difficult and sometimes impossible to observe accurately phenomena we do not understand.

Examples of Photographic Orientation

The orientation phase of a research project should give the researcher a sufficient grasp of a new culture so he *can* observe, identify, and relate. The language of a culture must be learned before we can see that culture in depth and compare one part of it to another. This visual learning might take weeks or months of valuable field time. Photography can facilitate this orientation experience. For example, in the Cornell Community Studies Program, Morris Opler provided his students with two years of study in the complex culture of India before they went overseas. A part of this orientation was a saturated exposure to photographs of Indian social roles, of priests, money-lenders, match-makers, and government officials.[1]

Visual orientation can be vital. During the Second World War the loss of pilots and planes of the Air Transport Command flying the Burma Hump to China was dangerously high. Pilots lost their way, planes ran out of gas and crashed, planes landed on enemy airfields. The weather conditions on the Burma Hump made visual orientation extremely difficult. Also one monastery looked like another; one mountain peak looked like another mountain peak. Every tool of briefing was used to cut down fatalities. The Command seized upon photography as one important tool of orientation and education. First a photoplane mapped the Burma Hump making continuous records, taken at the vantage of the pilot at normal flying altitudes. The negatives were enlarged to photomural proportions and hung around the walls of the briefing hut in Burma where pilots would be kept for hours at a time while they engraved the imagery of each view of the Burma Hump on their minds. Significant landmarks along the way had been carefully selected—lamaseries, valleys, rivers, airfields—every point that the pilot might quickly see to discover where he was. Even in tremendous clouds, through one opening in the mist a mountain peak might emerge to orient the pilot so he would know exactly where he was on the route.

There is necessarily a time lag in developing familiarity with a strange culture. A "first view of strangers" taken with a camera can allow the newcomer to an alien culture to make accurate records of an environment of which he has little knowledge. Complex cultural detail can be photographed without precise understanding. Interviewing native specialists with these first records allows for rapid identification and orientation. Photographs used in this way can teach the newcomer the visual language of a new culture.

As an example of this visual problem solving, consider the experience of Michael Mahar,[2] now teaching in the Oriental Studies program at the University of

---

[1] Private communication.
[2] Private communication.

Arizona, when he first arrived in India for fieldwork as a Cornell graduate student. One of Mahar's goals was to chart the social structure in one neighborhood of a large Indian village by tracking social interaction in the lanes, residential compounds, and during weddings attended by several hundred people. Who talked to whom? Who stopped where? The problem necessitated writing down repetitive observations at key points of sociometric movements and then relating this scheme to the community social structure. Immediately he had grave problems. He knew only a few of the villagers by name in the early phase of his fieldwork, and he could not readily ask for the identity of individuals in large groups without creating suspicion. It was evident that it would take him months to learn the identity of all the residents of the neighborhood, and visitors from other areas might not be recognized as such. Spontaneously he reached for the camera in hopes of solving his dilemma.

Mahar soon gathered a comprehensive view of the lanes and gathering places. When he was sure he had recorded the image of each resident, he took his records to a key informant in the community who easily identified each person. This intelligence was then used in conjunction with census materials to construct a code that indicated the social and spatial position of each resident of the neighborhood. Attention could then be given to the selective process of when and where to record. He could leave identification to his future laboratory study to come later, two or even five years away, when he would again use his photographic key to complete his sociometric analysis.

A fine statement of how insights are built in the field and how the camera can teach is given by John Hitchcock.

> Complexity of response is the clue. The good anthropologist knows some significances and learns others by living with the people in the community. He records some of the things he regards as significant, using the camera. Then he can begin responding to pictures as well as to people and place. All taken together help him to see further significances. You must emphasize this complex two-step and feedback process.[3]

The Photographer: A Participant Observer

Consider the difficulties of the fieldworker exploring technological change in a Canadian fishing community. How much can one see and record of such a complex technology—of the subtleties that differentiate one fishing technique from another, and that represent technological changes in the industry, in fishing methods, in the character of boats, and in the technology of fish packing? How much time would go simply to learn the basic movements of this complex process, *fishing,* before any refinements of difference or change could be observed? For the fieldworker who has never experienced this industry long questioning would be needed to learn even the language of fishing.

Measure this against the fieldworker from some similar maritime culture, who would come prepared with a spontaneous recognition, who could single out

---

[3] Private communication.

fine points related only to this area as compared to elements common to all Canadian fisheries. This fieldworker could immediately begin making pertinent observations significant to the study, while the first fieldworker would be spending weeks, if not months, mastering the language of the technology.

Consider a third circumstance where a novice fieldworker, who knows nothing about fishing but who is in command of a camera, approaches the technology with photography. Observation begins at five in the morning as the dragger fleet prepares to set to sea. In the misty light the community pier of the fishing port is filled with activity. The vessel our observer is to join lies below him, a maze of cables and lines and nets, which the crew are coiling and securing for sea. Coming down from the hills to the long pier the photographer makes a sweeping view of the harbor showing the vessels lying in the shelter along the pier inside the breakwater. He focuses on the activity of the people hurrying and lowering equipment into boats, groups of people standing together smoking. As he comes down the dock he makes an overhead view of the fishing boats, moored separately and sometimes three and four together along the pier.

As the fieldworker leans out over the vessel, the skipper hails him with "Here's the fellow who's going to take photographs, boys." The observer is introduced as someone who has a job to do; he will be as active as they are. A critical problem of role is solved by this introduction, "the fellow who's going to take photographs." The fieldworker's camera has played a part in this assignment from the very beginning. The skipper had been somewhat reluctant to take a greenhorn along. "We don't have time to answer a bunch of questions out there on the grounds; the wind's getting up and we're going to be pretty busy." When the fieldworker explained that he simply wanted to take photographs, the skipper's tone changed.

"Give the man a hand with his gear." The fieldworker jumps aboard the vessel and looks for a vantage point where he can keep out of the way and still see all that is going on. He settles on the deck of the pilot house and methodically films the as yet unexplained activity in the waist of the vessel. The steel chains of the dragger gear are shackled, tightened. Cables are wound onto winches. Lines are coiled and secured. One by one the vessels follow each other out of the breakwater, out into the bay, past lines of fish packing plants, fueling docks, yards, and warehouses. The fleet turns seaward, rounding a rocky headland, and meets the deep flow of the Atlantic. Astern the observer records the sweeping coastline, the rocky promontories, and the distinct patterns of farms and fields in the rising sun.

The routine of the vessel quiets; the crew relaxes awaiting the next phase of activity when they reach the grounds—a proper time for more formal introductions and explanations. "What are you taking these pictures for? Fun? Are you going to sell them to a magazine?" And the fieldworker is faced with his first important accomplishments—selling himself and explaining to the natives the purpose of his observations. Taking photographs is a reasonable activity, one which can be understood. Each time you take a picture your purpose is further recognized. Your ability to observe without asking many questions is vital in the circumstance where talking is difficult over the roar of the diesel engine and the critical activity of the crew.

Again, from his station on top of the pilot house the observer photographs the rapid sequence of lowering the drags and huge steel nets into the Atlantic. The engine slows, and the bottom of the sea is being swept for fish. It is a question of waiting, watching, and not asking. The vessel's engines stop, the boat rolls in the swells, and the screaming winches begin to haul a netload of fish from twenty fathoms of water. Activity quickens into a chaotic routine of lines, winches, and orders as the purse seine, streaming with water and burdened with hundreds of pounds of fish, is lowered down onto the dragger's deck. The purse is tripped and the deck is covered with many varieties of fish. Some are pitched overboard with a fork, others down into the icehold. Nets are rerigged and the dragging gear plunges again into the sea. Repetition of this activity over the day offers a very precise photographic record of technology. The crew becomes more involved in the observer's recordings; concerned that he capture each element of their trade, they begin offering him loud directions, "Stand by, now is the moment!" "Try it from the fo'c'sle head, you'll get a better view." This opportunity for cooperation, in which the native can tell the observer where to stand and what to see, creates a firm basis for rapport.

Afternoon sees the dragger fleet rounding the headlands and tying up to the packing plant wharf, each boat waiting its turn to unload its catch. The most sociable time of the day begins. The relaxation of waiting invites shouted conversations from boat to boat—friends, families, children, wives, managers of the packing plants, wharf hangers-on lean down from the wharf. The day's work is done. The catch is in.

"Are we going to get to see those photographs, Jack? Could we get some snaps?" The fieldworker is invited to come to call and bring his photographs. These invitations open a second and critical phase of the day's observations: the identification and reading of the photographs by the fishermen themselves. This opportunity brings to photographic orienation the control and authenticity that makes photographic exploration so valuable to anthropology.

The spontaneous invitation to the fieldworker to show his pictures is the result of a unique function of the camera in many kinds of studies. Informally we can call this photography's function as a "can-opener." The fieldworker, having spent one day recording on the dragger, has already introduced himself to the whole fishing community. Everyone knows who he is. Everyone has been told what he's been doing. Bridges of communication, established by the visual medium, can offer him rewarding collaborations within the field of study.

The fieldworker who photographed aboard the dragger can make a rapid entry in community research. "Will you show us the pictures?" can be his key to the homes of the dragger's crew. The first logical human step would be to call on the skipper who, when shown the pictures, is at once put in the role of the expert who teaches the fieldworker about fishing. The multiple details of the documents offer the captain an opportunity to express his knowledge and authority. He educates the fieldworker's untrained eyes with pictures of *his* boat, *his* crew, *his* skills.

This initial session of feedback can be very gratifying to the native, setting a strong identification with the stranger-observer. The skipper can become the fieldworker's champion, using the feedback pictures to add status to his position in the fishing community. After all, it was *his* boat that was chosen for study.

The evening's discussion of the photographs establishes a friendship with a community leader who can vouch for you and introduce you throughout the community. Your initial role is, "I'm the man who photographed Jim Hanks' dragger." The skipper in return must explain to friends and community who you are. After all everyone saw you photographing aboard his boat. Of course you must be a good person with an important mission, or your presence aboard would detract from the skipper's status.

Walking through the community with your new friend opens other opportunities. Entering the community proper by the side of an important fisherman is an excellent introduction. Have a glass with the skipper at the local store, and you will find yourself in the center of all his cronies. "Jack's the fellow who photographed my dragging." Here is a chance to talk casually of your study. Contacts are made—a foreman at the fish plant, the owner of the mercantile store—and your study can begin to fan out into the community at large. You have been introduced, your purpose factually understood, now you can proceed by various designs to gather the larger image of the community.

Of course we must recognize that the selection of collaborators is crucial, particularly in the early stages of fieldwork. As Patricia Hitchcock puts it:

> If a man's research plan involves the people he wishes to photograph he has to consider their feelings. He is not a tourist or press photographer whose aim often is to get a picture and get out, broken camera or no. Resentment of the camera can be overcome with the help of the right man—not the most willing man necessarily, who may be looking for attention, or who may be a deviant without the respect of the group—but a man who may have to be convinced the project is a valid one, a man who has power in the village and if possible the respect of all factions.[4]

This is also true with regard to choice of informants for interviewing; research goals must be pursued with realistic appreciation of social structure. The photographic fieldworker is especially concerned with these issues simply because his research takes place in full public view. Photography offers no covert methods for researching the community.

The photographer's role becomes even more critical when he is one of a team; what he does or does not do can jeopardize the whole research structure. His sensitive position stems from the role. Photographers are public figures, and the use of diplomacy and tact is of great importance in carrying through a community study. It is apparent that photography can either give the project a thoroughly negative introduction or provide community contacts that lay the foundation for extensive research, covering months or even years.

Because the native can grasp just what the photographer is doing and is therefore in a position to assist him, photography can provide a rapid entry into community familiarity and cooperation. The feedback opportunity of photography, the only kind of ethnographic note-making that *can* reasonably be returned to the native, provides a situation which often gratifies and feeds the ego enthusiasm of informants to still further involvement in the study. The concept of photography as a "can-opener" into human organizations has proved to be a sound one, *if* the re-

---

[4] Private communication.

search opens in a logical and sympathetic way, in terms of values of the native culture.

Dwight B. Heath, of Brown University, stumbled upon this rich possibility quite by accident while working, with Anna Cooper, on the ethnography of the Cambas near Santa Cruz, Bolivia. He prefers the metaphor "golden key" to "can-opener." He writes:

> The research design called for general recording of the technological and social culture of this lowland jungle area. Although the people were friendly enough, a dispersed settlement pattern of isolated homesteads and haciendas made systematic observations of many aspects of behavior difficult.
>
> Among our equipment we had a 35 mm camera and plenty of positive film, both color and black-and-white. Despite considerable delay and risk of loss, film was processed in the United States and returned to Bolivia where, in a casual gesture of friendship, a village priest once invited us to veiw our slides through his projector. The half-dozen bystanders were excited to see familiar people and places "in the movies," and told their friends. So many people asked to see the slides that a public showing was scheduled for an evening after church. More by popular demand than by design, a couple more showings drew ever larger audiences.
>
> At the same time that local people began affectionately (and a little proudly) to speak of "Ciné Camba," the feedback to us was becoming increasingly rich. The slide-shows thus became an enjoyable and informative weekly institution. Comments by the audience provided valuable attitudinal and conceptual data (in a sort of localized TAT [Thematic Apperception Tests] that might not otherwise have been elicited. Furthermore, we anthropologists took these occasions to explain our work briefly, and found an unexpected flood of goodwill and interest in our studies. It was probably not only in gratitude for the entertainment and excitement provided by the slide-shows, but also in the hope of appearing in them, that people began to give a virtual guide to each day's activities and to invite us to participate even in events that were normally restricted to a few kinsmen. Rites of passage, specialized techniques, and a host of other things that might otherwise have been missed were brought to our attention, and the camera became a "golden key" to anywhere.
>
> As interest and attendance increased at an almost exponential rate, the unexpected audience soon outgrew the patio of the churchyard. When a local farmer suggested that a suitable place for the showings be built, the priest offered to provide materials if the men would provide the labor. It was the first time in the memory of anyone in the area that a communal work project had been undertaken, but within a few weeks an area had been cleared and new benches doubled the former seating capacity. A whitewashed wall built as a projection screen was soon expanded upon to form a stage for school, church, and civic functions, and a surprising momentum carried over into a series of other voluntary public work projects.
>
> In this instance, an unusual use of visual ethnography not only resulted in goodwill and invitations that markedly increased our effectiveness as investigators, but also had the equally unforeseen value of fostering local community development.[5]

Many anthropologists have realistic anxieties about photographing freely in the cultural community, but experience has indicated that in many places of the world having one's image made with the camera can be a very gratifying experience,

---

[5] Private communication.

provided the native recognizes your view as a complimentary one. In many cultures documentation of human activity, technology, and social life, when photographed within the dimensions of protocol and human taste, can be a readily understandable form of investigation. It is an open form of recognition which people can thoroughly accept and understand, and the feedback of these documents of recognition proves to be a very stimulating experience.

Fieldworkers have found they can safely approach human organizations by operating in a logical sequence, *from the public to the most private,* from the formal to the informal, in a reasonable fashion from the outside in. The rule of thumb might be: photograph first what the natives are most proud of! In South America this might be the new water works, or the 300-year-old church. In the Maritimes of Canada it could be the dragger fleet, or prize oxen at the county agricultural fair. The general impression you can work toward is, "I like *you,* and I admire what *you* like." On the other hand, the minute you begin making records of circumstances which natives feel reflect criticism of their way of life, they can become dangerously hostile. In Mexico you can be arrested for photographing poverty. As the community's trust of you and an intelligent appreciation for your research increase, the natives will have a growing tolerance for what you choose to photograph. After all, what you photograph is *their* image and the nonverbal image often tends to be more emotionally charged than the one they express verbally and intellectually.

Speaking out of considerable experience with photography in the field, Patricia Hitchcock adds a particular note of caution in regard to feedback.

> We cannot assume that all people want to see themselves in pictures. We have to learn what they like to see. In some cultures pictures of people who have died turn the audience away. In a north India village wives are in purdah to protect them from outsiders. A husband would become very angry if you showed pictures of his wife to men outside the family. Even though village girls are permitted to dance outside the home on festival occasions, village elders would not like pictures of their daughters dancing shown to the public. Nice girls do not dance in public.[6]

Suspicion usually falls on the fieldworker when the native finds his operations irrational. Seeking a rationale for "Why is that man making all those pictures?" they can give the fieldworker the role of government spy, labor agitator, or worse. The man with the listening ear can pretend all kinds of reasons for his presence acceptable to the native, but when the photographer records slums down by the tracks, everyone in the community forms motives for the worker's photography. Hence, it is safer to leave the alleys to the last and start by photographing historical monuments and local dignitaries.

How to begin? Where to start? These are challenging questions in studying human societies by any method. Along with other anthropologists, photographers can follow the late Robert Redfield's advice to begin anywhere, and then move methodically from one relationship to another. Dr. Redfield suggested that village culture is an interrelated chain; keep pulling in and you will eventually handle all the links in this total relationship (1955:19).

> In moving to understand the systematic character of the life of a community the student cannot begin everywhere; he must begin at some point. Commonly the

---

[6] Private communication.

beginning is made with things immediately visible. . . . [Speaking of his study of Chan Com] I began where it happened to be convenient to begin. I went along with a man to the field he had cleared in the forest for the planting of his maize. I watched him cut poles and with them build a small altar in the field. I saw him mix ground maize with water and sprinkle it in the four directions, and then kneel in prayer. I watched him move across the field, punching holes in the shallow soil with a pointed stick and dropping a few grains of maize in each hole.

This entry led Redfield's observations over the trails that finally converged in the village, and then through streets that ended in the farmer's home where his wife and children lived. This simple journey inward tied together a countless multitude of visible details into one systematic relationship.

Redfield suggests various journeys through the culture, each of which would set up the symmetry of a whole concept—the biographic view, the journey of a man through his life, this endless chain would draw in all the cultural relationships of this village of Chan Com. He suggests the means to the whole are persistence and consistency, a patient threading of beads into a necklace. Photographically, the passage of one day with all the members of a family, would in itself be a synchronized view of the whole, offering a sensible place for thousands of details that might never be considered in whole relationships without some functioning scheme of human passage.

3

Photographing the Overview

T HE FIRST PHASE of fieldwork usually includes a variety of descriptive operations, outlining the shape of the culture to form a frame of reference within which the structured research goals can be accomplished. Usually this involves a mapping and sketching in of the environmental areas. Here the camera serves a second logical function.

Surveying and Mapping

When we think of photography as a tool for mapping we, of course, think of aerial photography, for this is one of the most accepted uses of the camera. Refined techniques of both aerial photography and aerial photographic reading have been developed. These techniques are so precise that an accurate two foot measurement can be obtained from 75,000 feet. Interpretation of aerial photographs has been pushed further than any other application of this medium, simply because photography is instantly seized upon by mappers as an indisputably useful process. Indeed, today very nearly every square mile of the world has been put on film. So complete are the files of aerial surveys that major archeological investigations have been based upon them. Subsurface structures that are indiscernible at ground view, become strikingly clear when seen at 1500 or 2000 feet elevation, particularly when the rays of the sun are falling in the right direction. Site after site has been found in this way. Archeology, in England, Peru and elsewhere, owes a great deal to aerial photographic reconnaissance.

More recently aerial photographs have been used as a source of sociological data. Harvard University's Chiapas Project under the leadership of Evon Z. Vogt and George A. Collier, carried out major community investigations using photographic aerial reconnaissance. Charles Rotkin, a New York photographer who films from the air professionally, provided most of the photographs for a book on European village patterns as seen from low flying planes. These records have great his-

Field and home relationships in the Andes.

torical value and present ecological relationships almost impossible to grasp except with this kind of photographic reconnaissance (Egli 1960).

Petroleum exploration demonstrates the dynamic relationship of aerial photography to ground-level investigation. In the worldwide search for oil, photo-geology has become a highly developed field which allows exploration over very wide areas. Potential oil fields are examined first with aerial photographs. Photographs taken when the sun is at the proper angle reveal subsurface geology in the same way they reveal Viking tombs in the heaths of England. A highly developed interpretive technique allows geologists to project subsurface geology from the outcroppings that relate to structures thousands of feet below the surface. Then the petroleum geologist, like the archeologist, moves from aerial photographs to ground investigation. Ground parties study the outcroppings first hand. The field geologist carries the aerial photographs with him and usually begins his analysis by studying the aerial records with a stereoptic viewer before the survey crew analyzes the outcrops with geological compasses and transfers these readings directly onto a regional map with aid of a mapping transit. The Harvard Chiapas Project moved from aerial photographs to village studies in much the same fashion.

Aerial photography is supplemented by long views taken from whatever high points are present. Where aerial photos are hard to get, long vistas may serve as well, particularly if the area has already been mapped. Panoramas and dioramas, with a sweep of 180° are especially valuable. Ground-level sampling of the characteristic ecological features will help in the reading and interpretation of the aerial and long-view photos. Both color and black and white photographs reveal the altitude belts of agriculture and natural ecology. Color photographs, used with a color key for variety of soils, can rapidly indicate the geological topography of a whole farming region.

When we move from air to ground level mapping with the camera, our descriptive goals remain the same—to project onto the diagrammatic map the full detail of ecology and human activity. As an example, the U.S. Soil Conservation Service has relied heavily on the camera for ground mappings. The nature and quality of the terrain, the good and bad range recognizable in detailed records of grass and bush, the character of erosion by wind or water, can all be responsibly read from ground photographs and factually transferred from the photographic data to mapping overlays.

Variables of Ecology and Land Use Easily Read from Aerial and Long-View Photographs

Relation of agriculture to geographic features—how far out in the desert, how close to the sea, how far up the mountain.

Field patterns, large fields, small fields.

Land divisions by walls, hedges, fences.

Engineering of irrigation systems from water source to the fanning out of ditches.

Soil fertility—good land, poor land.

Rocky soil as compared to alluvial delta soil.

Water erosion—areas where soil has washed, or where alluvial movement has built soil.

Wind erosion.

Distribution of rock-strewn fields.

Fields plowed with rocks in situ (technology necessarily with hand tools; mechanized agriculture would be impossible).

Fields cleared of rocks, large stone piles and stone fences bespeaking effort.

Agricultural technology—use of contour plowing, understanding of soil conservation in irrigation, plowing to retard erosion or without regard for it, presence or absence of terracing.

Proportion of farmlands that are going back into brush and forests.

Forest growth.

Timber cutting and timber farming operations.

Areas of forest blight.

The Photographic Shape of Community Designs

If an anthropologist could hover over a community in a balloon what would he observe of community design? Foremost would be the community's ecology; desert community, sea coast community, forest community, crowded city neighborhood, isolated rural town. Beyond these geographic considerations the fieldworker would want to conceive of the community as a kind of organism. The small American town has its main street, around which the town is often structured; the Mexican community has its central plaza; Pueblo Indian communities used to nestle on mesas for self-protection.

Villages in diverse environments often have distinct designs—sometimes related to ecology, sometimes a product of culture. Aerial photographs of Europe show intense concentration of cities to reserve space for farmlands. Are technology and super populations breaking down this traditional conservation? Breaking down by what pattern? The patterned spread of habitations out into the open lands is revealed distinctly in both aerial and panoramic photographs.

French communities in Nova Scotia are strikingly different from English communities, yet they share similar ecology. In photographs it is possible to define the space between houses, the French clinging to a village pattern even though the village street may be 5 miles long. The English, who are more individually oriented, scatter their communities loosely over their respective farmsteads. Each culture uses land in a particular way; the differences may be subtle, yet the patterns divide one people from another. This is common knowledge, but specific measurements and comparisons will help establish this character responsibility in anthropology. Photography of the designs of communities, from the air and the ground, provide a basis for such measurement and comparison.

A first photograph of the community could be the panoramic view, ideally matching panoramic views that would give us several 180° sweeps of the full pattern of the village and its surroundings. Is the community centralized? Or is it scattered? A fishing community might be built near docks and around harbors. As we enter the community with the camera we ask again the question of economic status, and though the question grows more complex, many nonverbal variables still remain on the surface, allowing us to rate the town regionally or examine the town individually for its own divisions of poverty and affluence. Conspicuous consumption becomes an important variable and one that can be recorded with the camera. We ask is this community economically a hub of the region? Has the town a lively mercantile center? What are its major offerings—feed, fertilizer, or ship chandlery supplies? Photographically we attempt to record every bit of propaganda and advertising—political, cultural, and commercial. We photograph to count how many and how large are the stores. If we photograph on a shopping day we can observe how popular this center is as compared to nearby villages, how many cars are parked on the streets, how many people are coming and going.

Beyond the physical and economic schemes of the town there remains its well-being and cultural vitality. Any park benches to rest on? Bandstand for concerts and gatherings? Is the town dominated by Catholicism or by many splinter Protestant churches? Are there places of recreation—bars, restaurants, movie theaters?

Photographing strictly in the public domain, the camera can gather in a few hours' visit the *outer face* of the community, and some major outcroppings of regional culture as well, again provided we seek reliable variables of measurements and comparisons. Many elements in this community visit are discernible as well with your eyes, but how can written notations preserve the wide variety of ecological impressions? And how precisely? How will you compare your field notebook records made in one locale to those made in another? Or geographically to other regions which might contain comparable environment? How comparable? Impressions gained with the eye alone grow dim, fuse with other impressions, and with time fade away. When you use the camera it is possible to assemble a very complex model which contains literally thousands of tangible elements to be compared to other communities photographed throughout the region.

We turn to government maps and geophysical charts because of their dependable character. This allows for an even reading of data by students of diverse disciplines. Photographic mapping and surveying increase the dimensions of detail of these geophysical charts, and enable us to relate ecology definitively to culture, social structure, and technology.

Photographic profiles of communities, both rural and urban, can be transferred to the conventional diagrammatic map either in overlays or with colored pins. The goal of our efforts is to use the intelligence of photographic mapping to relate ethnographic considerations to the larger ecology. The concept of overlays can be extended to include many visible schemes of community culture, as well as such variables as affluence and poverty and housing types.

The mapping of these characteristics was attempted in Cornell's Stirling County Study in the Maritimes of Canada directed by A. H. Leighton. The field team's first attempt to gather their data for an affluence and poverty mapping overlay indicated how important photography can be in this kind of surveying. In the project's first attempt to gather data teams of fieldworkers, two to a car, toured the area. Roads, yards, sizes of houses, conditions of repair were checked off appropriately on a dittoed form as they drove down the country lanes. In this test run teams were paired against each other and, to the discouragement of all, the evaluations of the housing did not agree. Fieldworkers quite naturally rated housing against their own environmental background; a fieldworker from the country would treat the houses one way, while a fieldworker from an urban environment would evaluate them in another way. The result was quite a range of impressions. In an effort to stabilize this operation, I went into the same area as the project photographer, making Leica shots of houses down one side of the road and up the other. These were enlarged to 8 by 10 in. and presented to the evaluation team who sat in a circle and passed the photographs—rating each one of the houses on the back. Again, the discrepancy of judgments was far too great, but now the operation had a powerful control—photographs. They were laid on the floor and argued over until the judgments were finally agreed upon and the criteria for rating affluence and poverty in housing were responsibly established. The field team then went about making their survey. The survey could have been completed by photographic reconnaissance, with a group-judging of the housing photos which would have given the added advantage of a permanent file record. In the course of the continuing research, I recorded several whole rural communities, each in a matter of hours. This material was shown to key informants who were able to give instructive information about every home in one interview. This offered a responsible source of community mapping and personality identity, obtained without a house-to-house questionnaire (Collier 1957).

Photographs can become more intelligible to the researcher when the precise visual symbols of interpretation are systematically recognized. In both rural and urban surveys, measurements that allow for anthropological typologies are not just graphic impressions. Instead they are pinpointed observations of variables that can be responsibly counted, measured, and qualified.

Mapping affluence and poverty in rural areas operates around a few visual norms which have psychological, cultural, and economic significance. Starting from the simplest dimensions, we have the absolute comparisons of large homes and small homes, and of run down homes and well kept homes. How commodious the houses? How many stories? How many outbuildings? Photographs allow for exacting comparison of scale. When we move further into culture, economic level may become just one of the factors to be noted in the charting of regional mental health. Emotional and cultural well-being, can also be recognized in photographs of dwellings. (Qualities of order and disorder suggest various emotional states, such as integration or chaos in acculturation.)

Some Variables of Well-Being in a Rural Setting

ECONOMIC

> Fences, gates and driveways
> Mail boxes, labeled, painted
> Telephone lines

Power lines to house, to outbuildings
Condition of house walls and roof
Condition of windows
Condition of yard, flower beds, or vegetable garden
Farm equipment near house
Trucks and cars in yard

CULTURAL AND PSYCHOLOGICAL
Intrinsic care of the house
Decorative painting
Curtains in windows, potted plants
Self-expression in garden: abundance of flowers
Self-expression in yard: raked, swept, wood and tools stacked and stowed, or
    property scattered about

Variables for recognizing psychological levels would have to be put together within the value system of the region under study. Each culture has its own signposts of well-being. When these signs are understood, a photographic survey gives the opportunity for rich interpretations.

The question of how can we arrive at these variables is immediately raised. Briefly, we can standardize cross-cultural nonverbal language through projective interviewing with environmental photographs. This procedure will be covered in depth in a later chapter.

Designs of the city offer the community research project even greater visual challenges, for the units involved run into thousands. Door to door questioning and census material form the basis of much urban anthropological mapping. When samples of streets are photographed evidence for mapping increases. In one of my courses at San Francisco State College students used this approach in mapping a complex urban neighborhood in the city of San Francisco. The fieldworkers divided up the area by streets, and proceeded to photograph angle views from the top of each street to the bottom so that all the houses were viewable in the photographs. The mapping area started in the affluent foothills of Twin Peaks and dropped down into the marginal industrial area of the Mission District. From the photographs, the movement and the condition of housing was established and transposed to a city map. The areas of recent construction rested in the foothills; below were older homes remodelled, older homes in good repair, older homes in deteriotrated condition, housing areas invaded by industry, areas completely dominated by industry. Each street yielded its precise measurement. Each fieldworker's photographs were placed on the wall and the group as a whole agreed on the reading. In this way, the research team mapped the housing patterns of the area, bringing to this study refinements unobtainable on the census and appraisers' records. The control factor offered by such photographic reconnaissance can be of great support to scientific findings. The readability of photographic evidence allows for a rapid cross-check of field workers' judgments and stabilized statements can be assembled from the group evaluation.

The Range of Photographic Observation

As can be seen from the examples we have considered, the cycle of fieldwork moves swiftly from the larger areal dimensions to a closer look at the details of culture, moving, as it were, from the mass of the forest to the examination of the varieties of trees and leaves. Histories, folk stories, myths, and various methods of interviewing may all be explored for significant data. At this stage of the research, much of the questioning is necessarily open-ended. Although we may know quite a bit about the more formal structure, social change and conflicting elements require us to take a fresh look at what is actually happening. The value of photography in this circumstance is that it offers unique ways of looking at and describing culture which can provide new clues to the significance of the variables.

The question we raise in the general effort at description, with or without the camera, is how fluent should your sense of evidence be in order to gather meaningful open-ended data? Should you think in terms of how your collected evidence might be used? Should you have a reliable language of what *can* be intelligently observed, audially or visually? In other words, is there a language and a recognizable meaning in evidence that can be learned, so that data that goes into the file can be fitted into a sensible scheme?

Fieldworkers do not write down everything they observe. That would be impossible. What do they write down? By what system do they select? Obviously they record against various structured designs of significance, influenced by their training and the formal goals of the research so that what they record forms a significant pattern. We can say this is also true in photographic recording.

By what process do we make *significant* photographs? What types of nonverbal evidence are computable? The scientifically readable content of photographs will necessarily suggest how and when to record.

Paul Byers, anthropologist-photographer, presents a sound scheme that can give the photographer the role of the extended vision of the research project. The project might have a team of photographers observing for them. The plan seems to me to come out of the very craft of photo-reportage in which cameramen, knowing they cannot document everything, tend to work in prescribed areas with an informal but structured list of of objectives to insure holistic coverage. First, Byers works intensely with the scientist for whom he is going to observe, absorbing the objectives of the study and the needs of data. Second, out of these insights he forms a frame of reference, that I would loosely call a shooting script, and "takes hundreds of still photographs around these points of significance." This means he observes intensely with the goals of the study in mind. Third, he assembles the field photographs into orderly structures, also built around the frame of study. Finally, the scientist studies this data and coordinates the nonverbal evidence with his developing research. Such an assignment might record a micro-culture or the scope of a geographic region—a day's photography or 2000 to 6000 negatives made over a year's field period. Describing Byers' work, Margaret Mead points out that, "The success of this approach depends more on the understanding of the researcher's framework and the translation of some part of this to still photographic recording than on the improvement or elaboration of photographic techniques per se." (Mead 1963:178–179)

Photography is a process of abstraction; we never construct anything approaching a complete document. In any practical sense, photography is *very* selective. Throughout a day's field recording only a minute time sample can be or is recorded. If this is the case, how much of the photographic image *can* be used for research? Before we proceed further, these problems should be examined or we will have difficulty in planning and carrying out our hypothetical field examination.

How much of a photograph can we use in direct research? As anthropology's recognition of nonverbal evidence expands, there is no predicting how completely photographs may be processed into data. In the meantime, we can responsibly use selected elements which can be read out of photographs and translated into research conclusions. As we consider the abstracting process of the vast detail contained in photographs, it will help to keep in mind the basic uses of photographs in research: *counting, measuring, comparing, qualifying,* and *tracking.* Most photographic evidence which has found practical use in direct research can be examined under one or more of these five categories.

We return to the field study to suggest the scope of photographic content. Counting and measuring are the most immediate applications of the automative recording of photography. Measuring is a realistic basis for surveying and charting; counting opens an even wider door to the cultural inventory. How much? How often? How complex? These are documentary qualifications that allow for precise evaluation and comparison. Tracking means sociometric measuring, the drift of social structure that flows and overlaps in community culture. The community study offers us a simplified frame within which to examine both the application and content of these nonverbal elements.

The most accepted use of the camera has been to describe objects that because of their stationary character offer a responsible impression. We pick up counting and measuring at the point of practical examination of not only the physical sciences but also archeology. For decades the archeological technicians have been making precise in situ photographs to measure placement of burials, and in museums have been comparing photographs of one artifact against another. In anthropology we move forward from this point, bearing in mind that the key that will unlock the cultural trove from photographs is the same as the control over impressionism.

The shape of culture certainly contains endless components that are as unchanging and at the same time as voiceless as the relics of archeology. The past cannot speak, and accordingly archeological methodology employs deductions drawn from nonverbal evidence. In anthropology much of the shape of culture remains equally nonverbal, though this visual image may be glossed over for lack of systematic description.

Colombian mestizo spinner. The delicacy of this highly skilled ancient process makes it hard for the eye to follow or the memory to reconstruct. Photographs fix the image for realistic analysis and reappraisal.

4

Photographing Technology

THERE IS no more logical subject for photography than native technology, Craft and industry are the means by which people survive in an environment, and would appear to the native as *the* most important areas to start a study. Here is the heart of anxiety and pride. "The draggers are ruining the fishing." "The trees are giving out." "Anyone who can build a boat can build a barn. We're woodworkers from way back. We can all build our own homes. . . ." Photographing technology means photographing economy, but also more. Technological change may be the most basic acculturation, and the death of an industry may spell the decline of a culture.

Comprehensive documentation of a technological process is practical and extremely rewarding in ethnography. This is another example of Redfield's concept of the whole, for when we record all the relationships of a technology we have, in many circumstances, recorded one whole view of a culture. It is difficult to disassociate a people's means of livelihood from their symbiotic relationship with ecology and their social structure or their value system. This may be less clear in an industrial society where life's goals are fragmented, but often in a peasant society the whole of culture is held together by the technology.

As we have said, a major problem is learning enough about the technology so we *can* meaningfully observe it. Cross-culturally this can be a challenge, for the significance of a craft is embedded in the very ethos of a culture. Swiftly moving technologies are particularly hard to understand and document.

The value of the camera in these circumstances has already been suggested. Using the camera with reasonable discipline the inexperienced fieldworker can record with accuracy the operations of a sawmill, even when he has a shallow grasp of what is going on. Saturated recording, especially with the 35 mm camera, makes it possible to follow technological sequence in great detail. On first examination these records may be too complex for a reasonable understanding, but they can be restudied later when the fieldworker is adequately oriented. Or if precise information is needed at once, the native specialist, away from the frenzied activity of the mill, can read the photographs giving precise names and functions for the record. Thus, an encyclopedic understanding of an otherwise bewildering operation is obtainable.

When technological photographs have been read and identified in this fashion, the fieldworker is able to study his documents independently with an increasing opportunity for research within the details of the photograph. He can observe the characteristic position of personalities in the industrial circumstance, whether these be laborers or foremen. The repetitious human positions invite the writing of a complete and precise description supported by the imagery of the photographs.

What skills do you need to photograph how a man makes a canoe? Or how he catches a fish, or harvests his wheat? Your goals in recording are two-fold: the step-by-step craft operation; and the relationship of the industry to the total culture. The first goal is achieved by comprehensive sampling, the second by an expansive scheme of observation.

Keeping abreast of a fast-moving process requires more command than taking snapshots of your native host's children, but mastery of the camera does not insure a good coverage. A box camera effort might be superior to the virtuoso's effort, if a sound scheme of observation is used. The fine technological record is made by alertness and patience. If a technology repeats, stand back and study it. Analyze what appear to be the various peaks of activity, when tools are changed or technology varies. If the process is baffling, make a saturated record and with the help of a specialist pick out the key steps. In this way you will quickly acquire an authoritative functional understanding of even an unfamiliar industry.

A Scheme of Observation

ENVIRONMENTAL LOCATION OF THE TECHNOLOGY
> Forest-ringed sawmill
> Desert-surrounded farmer
> City-congested craft center

RAW MATERIALS IN THE SHOP
> Hewn wood
> Earth for clay
> Metal for forging

TOOLS OF THE TRADE: AN INVENTORY OF TECHNOLOGY
> Plows of metal
> Plows of wood
> Digging sticks
> Hooks, nets, and harpoons
> Floats and traps
> Tools of stone, bone, or wood for chipping, piercing, and pounding
> Tools of metal for gouging, cutting, hammering, etc.

HOW TOOLS ARE USED
> Show each tool's support of the technology
> Show how tools are cared for and stored; this can be as vital a part of the
> culture of technology as the shape of the finished product

HOW A CRAFT PROCEEDS

Logs drawn from the millpond
Ground furrowed for planting
Ground pierced for seeding
Wool fluffed for carding
The first cuts of the craftman's chisel
Mound of clay on the potter's wheel
The first coil of clay for a bowl

CONCLUSION OF PROCESS

The bowl is drawn from the kiln or firing
The kachina doll is completely painted
Timber has been cut into boards and stacked
The corn has been husked and stored

THE FUNCTION OF TECHNOLOGY

What do the weavers use textiles for?
How are kachina dolls used?
What does silver do for the Navajos?
Do the fishermen eat their fish?

SOCIAL STRUCTURE IN TECHNOLOGY

What are the relative degrees of skill?
What are the most skilled jobs?
What are the most dangerous assignments?
What are the skills of the people of prestige?
What is the lowest status job in the mill?

The larger relationships of a technology require us to photograph not only the process, but also the source of raw materials and later the cultural end of the created product. Otherwise we will not have an integrated view of native skills.

Technology is one area where acculturation can be observed. Hence, it is particularly important to examine tools. They should be photographed so a precise comparison with like tools in another culture is possible. We must be equally alert to the ways in which tools are used, because sometimes in acculturation new tools are adapted to unchanging archaic processes. Use may change more slowly than the adoption of new materials and artifacts in many circumstances.

Understanding the use of craft and manufacture is an integral part of a technological study. In this phase we observe the function of the craft in the culture. Is one culture technologically superior to another because the items it manufactures for trade are more complex? Or superior because their technology allows them to live more fruitfully in their environment? A culture might show a very high level of skill in the production of ceramics or textiles, yet not involve these products in daily living. By tracking technology's manufacture into the culture its integration in daily life can be evaluated.

In Newfoundland the major craft is fishing, yet the natives suffer severe malnutrition because they do not eat much fish. Instead fish is traded for poor quality canned meat from South America. One result is the high incidence of false teeth even among young Newfoundlanders.

Roles in technology often define the social structure. In the villages of India many work roles are dictated by caste. In the Maritimes of Canada status is held by "high-line" fishermen, the most skilled men in the fishing community. Work assignments in structured communities establish one's place in the society, and mobility is a function not only of accumulating wealth but also of a higher place in the prestige system of skills. In the community technological enterprise, in the operations of the fishing dragger or the sawmill in the forest, each technological job should be carefully recorded so that later, through photographic reading, personality identification can be made and workers' positions in the structure considered. This social record of skills allows you to perceive where to look for status. The native photographic reader can help interpret the social significance of skills.

Very often in a limited field period, the observer is faced with the negative circumstance in which an important link in the seasonal technology has past—you cannot photograph haying in the spring. But there are many craft technologies that can be carried out at any time at the request of the fieldworker. "We make our lobster nets in the fall before the season hits." "Can you show me how to make them now?" Craft is sufficiently ritualistic so the craftsman conscientiously carries out an operation in the traditional manner. There is only one way to knot a lobster net, only one correct way to set a coyote trap. With the aid of the camera very exact models of native technology can be gathered in the same way we interview. "Tell me how you feed the stock in winter," is just a more abstract way of asking, "Show me how." The late Samuel A. Barrett of the University of California at Berkeley made most of his ethnographic footage in just this way, in acted out interviews.

A process must be photographed so exact steps can be isolated. It is by this systematic observation that a technology can be conceived functionally.

For the follow-through of a process film is suggested as a fluent medium. In our Western culture the motion picture camera is a very stimulating tool for acting out all manner of circumstances, whether in sociodrama or in carrying through a craft. If you had enough film and *could* keep the camera going for the full duration of a process through hours, days, and weeks, indeed you would have the unbroken sequence. In effect you would have essentially unaltered reality, that would be as unwieldy for analysis as the raw circumstance. Photography is an abstracting process, and as such is in itself a vital step in analysis. So when we photograph, consider that we are involved in refinement. It is seldom practical to make an unbroken film document even of a simple technology, because of the relationships and time span involved. Whether we use a Leica camera or a movie camera we must still *sample* and structure the whole view around significant time slices that demonstrate the continuity of a process.

The still camera can also stimulate people to act out a process and has some advantages over the movie camera, including facility of feedback. We have the instant pictures of the Polaroid Land camera, but we also can exploit the relatively fast return of the conventional camera, even though the contact prints may be small. Feedback in the technological circumstance has proved to be very stimulating to the native craftsman provoking him to refine and make very complete enactments of

An Andean Indian craftsman combines European technology and Pre-Columbian skill. Only refined comparisons of many textile processes can be counted upon to indicate which elements are Indian, which European. Otavalo weaver, Ecuador.

technology, the point being that the feedback of photographs allows him to share in the progress of the study as he sees the documents of his skill.

An ideal research occurrence of this kind took place during our study of the weaving culture of the Otavalo Indians in Ecuador (Collier and Buitron 1949). We were faced with the problem of having incomplete knowledge about the technology of this area. This was coupled with a rapport problem, for the Otavalo weavers were somewhat uncooperative about being photographed, in some degree because of a sense of magic danger in the photography, or more likely from a sense of being exploited by the gringo. A solution to this dilemma was found when we were introduced to a master weaver of the area. We asked him if he would weave us the yardage for a suit. This offer was enthusiastically accepted as we bargained for a price during the early Sunday market. We seized this circumstance as the key to our research and explained to the weaver that because of peculiar circumstances it would be necessary to photograph our tweeds being woven, and that we wanted to follow our suiting from the raw wool to the finished cloth. The Indian looked with puzzlement, and possibly annoyance, at this unusual request, and thinking it over, said in effect, "Well, it is your suit. You can do what you please!"

A date was made to call on our collaborator to witness the first part of the textile process—the washing, the drying, and the carding of the raw wool. Our welcome at the Indian's home was perfunctory, but the weaver proceeded swiftly to carry through the process of preparing the wool for carding, while we recorded the activity with a Rolleiflex camera.

We developed the film immediately in our field laboratory, made contact prints, and returned with cameras and contacts a few days later.

The weaver greeted us with some surprise as we handed him the proofs of our photographs. His knowledge of photography was limited to portrait photography done in the Otavalo Plaza. He spread the contact prints out on the ground, arranged the pictures in technological sequence, and surveyed our results. He stood up, shook his head in disappointment, and made it clear that we had not done a good job on his craft. And more, he said, he was very concerned that the world would see him in these photographs as a poor weaver. He insisted that we repeat the process, so each step could be more plainly shown and with more honor to him. (He had neglected to keep his hat on, a major status symbol in Otavalo.) He made it clear that this time he would let us know *when* to take the pictures. The process was duplicated much more slowly and with great care. When we returned with our prints a second time, he accepted them with approval, and we proceeded on to the other steps, carding, spinning, and dying the yarn, and finally weaving the cloth.

We continued to feedback all the pictures we made and the Indian weaver took a key role in directing and organizing how the technology was to be recorded. He so identified with our study that by the end of the cloth he said, "There are many kinds of weaving that you have not photographed that other Indians do. I will go with you and see that these pictures are made. These men are doing weaving for me which I will sell, and they will have to let you take pictures."

The cooperation of our Indian collaborator allowed us to make a study of the Otavalo textile industry more complete than we ever could have made if we had tried to direct the course of this photographic coverage. This can be spoken of as an acted out interview stimulated by the feedback of photographs. Whether in a fishing boat off the coast of Canada or in a forest sawmill, or with an Indian weaver in Ecuador, if the subjects of a study have the initiative of organizing and informally directing the fieldworker's observing experience, the result can be a very complete and authentic record.

To be sure, one may have to pick and choose among native technologists to find a craftsman to collaborate with in this way. But a similar degree of rapport is needed for any form of depth investigation, and involvement is a major element in rapport. As Oscar Lewis says of the family in the foreword to *Children of Sanchez,*

> Their identification with my work and their sense of participation in a scientific research project, however, vaguely they conceived of its ultimate objectives, gave them a sense of satisfaction and of importance which carried them beyond the more limited horizons of their daily lives (1961:xxi).

5

Photographing Social Interaction

THE PHOTOGRAPHING of social actions leads us into a rich area of nonverbal research. A considerable variety of reliable evidence can be read from photographs of social scenes, for we find in them the complex dimensions of social structure, cultural identity, and psychological expression. Pictures of people mingling offer us opportunities for measuring, qualifying, and comparing, but these measurements can go much further and help define the very shape of social culture.

Many aspects of social structure are readily discussed in verbal interviews, for people feel they know their place in the social strata. To experience these social levels visually, we must observe natives acting out their roles. Who speaks to whom? Who goes where? And when? Who goes to the late Saturday night movie? Who gathers and comes from bars and cocktail lounges? Keeping track of these movements with our eyes alone requires astute observations. Juxtaposition of people must be recognized and memorized in a flash, and personalities must be accurately perceived. This takes time and considerable familiarity. With the camera this task can at many points, become a fairly automatic operation, and can be accomplished without advance understanding.

The city streets can be a practical laboratory for photographic analysis of social phenomena. All through the complex interrelationships of urban culture photographic tracking takes on statistical significance in computer oriented analysis of mass populations. The cultural, economic, and racial characteristics of urban areas can be examined in the ebb and flow of city thoroughfares. This flow of population, spontaneously performing, and realistically grouping, is a monolithic social structure in motion. Bus stops and cross-walks are like the waterholes and trails in the jungles: wait patiently, and all the forest life will pass before you. Photo-journalist W. Eugene Smith stalked the city of New York by keeping a telephoto lens trained on 6 feet of pavement on the corner of 18th Street and Sixth Avenue. Over a period of a year, as he worked on a book, he shot frame upon frame of street culture. Beggars, lovers meeting, drunken fights, muggings, snow in winter, cloud bursts in summer, all came to his 6 feet of paving (Smith 1958).

Photographs of one car stop from early morning to night in a scheduled de-

A church supper in a rural community in the Maritimes of Canada. This record is a key to the social culture, the inter-relationships that reach far out from this isolated settlement. Family ties and community alliances are re-established at this annual summer gathering.

sign will tell you many things about a city neighborhood. Who goes to work at seven every morning—Negroes, Orientals, Caucasians? Men and women poorly dressed, well dressed? Who takes the bus at eight in the morning? How many school children? How many office workers with gray flannel suits and brief cases? How many women? How many men? How young and how old? All this through the use of photographic detail, can be classified into rough scales of affluence and poverty, or analyzed for social roles, occupations, or functions. Over the period of a week the statistical evidence is impressive and can yield reliable profiles of neighborhood structure.

The mingling of people on the city streets can roughly classify most urban communities. In New York City there is an inverse relationship between affluence and the number of people on the streets. The more poverty, the more the city dwellers flee to the openness of the pavement. Crowds of people on the streets of a residential area mean small rooms and overcrowding. Each city community has touch points where the character of its populace can be tracked and measured, the mingling in front of supermarkets, libraries, coming and going from churches, and relaxing in city parks. All these are key points where social flow can be documented and where social structure can be observed in motion.

Whether in a rural center or in a city neighborhood, fieldworkers working through one Sunday can reasonably characterize the religious affiliations of the community, by photographing the arrival and dispersal of the various church congregations. The lone fieldworker could accomplish this same study over a series of Sundays. The interlocking movement of the social structure could be determined by this technique. Who runs the town's bazaars? Who hosts the church suppers? The participant fieldworker can systematically observe all the community gatherings in this fashion, see the leaders in their roles, and with the help of a native, establish the personality associations with accuracy.

Recording what people look like, what they wear, and the condition of their clothes is a descriptive opportunity offering rich clues to identifications comparable to those provided by exteriors and interiors of homes. Records of clothing can be rated as satisfactorily as can the conditions of roofs and yards. Ethnographically, clothing provides evidence for the comparison of ethnic groups and social organizations, defines roles of the rich and the poor, and differentiates the rural dweller from the city dweller. A saturated statistical view of garments can reveal cultural characteristics as much as can the property of the home.

The single observation, like the single photograph, of a social demonstration holds only a few points of reliable data. One photograph, like the one ethnographic visit, tells only the way life is *right now*. Evaluation is static, dealing with a possibly arbitrary schematic position. It is not open to the qualification of change. How many people are present? Where are they all standing at one fixed time? What is going on at this exact moment? One sample view is strictly empirical. But when we speak of social structure, we speak of patterned behavior recurring through time. It takes multiple views to observe what is the *customary behavior* as compared to eccentric behavior.

When time and motion records are added to the image of social interaction we have the opportunity to examine the ebb and flow of gatherings. The camera offers us time slices that can be measured and added to time sweep. Various time-span interactions can be measured and compared, interaction of minutes, hours, days, weeks, and even a full year, can be calculated from timed observations of the flow of life on the village street.

The camera's great value is that it *can* make a repetitive record, covering many combinations of intervals. When interaction is examined repetitively, schemes are solidified into organic patterns—ebbing, flowing, gathering and dispersing—which tie interaction into the multiple cause-and-effect relationships of a culture.

As an example, a student made timed records of campus noon hour political assemblies in hopes of defining a pattern of gathering. On first glance, the results were chaotic. There did not seem to be a strong pattern or an impressive definition—rather there were multitudes of small changes. The student then related his time lapses to three factors: (1) the time factor of class schedules; (2) time lapses related to who was speaking, (3) the subject of each speaker. When the photographs were enlarged and examined in their precise time association, the suggestive photographic patterns of students running to and from the gathering, groups breaking away and dispersing, sudden influx of students arriving, all began to take on intelligible schemes.

Detailed study at this point reflected patterns in listening, bodies pressing forward as the content log revealed a certain student had the floor; then in other photos, students would be turning away, laughing to one another as the content of the debate changed again. When the gathering was correlated to class schedules, still another crowd movement became discernible. On closer view, when students simply drifted off for lack of interest there appeared to be a different pattern than when students were breaking from the crowd to go to class. In the latter case students either left on the run, or showed their reluctance, listening, heads turned to the crowd, as they moved away.

Sociometric Observations of Social Structure

A wide variety of units within urban sociology present problems of observation and understanding: the social structure of the monolithic office organization, the structure of industrial plants, mobility and status within unions. Arthur Rotman, as a project for a field method seminar at San Francisco State College, attempted to define the social structure of a hospital staff and observe the nature of race relations (1964). But hospitals have their own taboos and a staid hierarchy of roles and customs. Hospitals are also an aseptic facade of white coats and regulations. Where to begin? Whom to interview? What to ask? In search of the real structure and interaction, Rotman sought a circumstance of common ground, with maximum fluency, in hopes of observing the spontaneous groupings of social structure and human relations.

The point of observation selected was the hospital cafeteria—the method of observation was photography. Methodologically, the choice involved three field problems: (1) the time factor of balanced interviewing throughout the structure was prohibitive; (2) protocol made interviewing within the hospital itself dangerous if not impossible; (3) the pace of life and the probable hierarchical lines would make asking questions on the intersocial structure difficult. The captured locale of the lunchroom would allow observation of the social structure in motion in a controlled fashion. Rotman's role was that of participant observer, for he worked at the hospital and also wore a white coat. The study was made with the permission of the director.

Rotman's technique was a time-and-motion study made at fifteen minute intervals every day for a week from nine positions that gave him a record of all the staff throughout the lunch period. Completing his sample involved meeting with some individual agitation, but without serious offense. The costumes worn by all hospital staff members allowed for responsible identification of each individual's position. Nurses' aides, trained nurses, x-ray technicians, and other specialists wore emblems and written identifications. Doctors wore stethoscopes. Surgical aides wore green coats.

The photographs were made with 35 mm film with a wide angle lens. Thirty-five millimeter film is all edge-numbered and offered further control for the analysis of the time and motion factors of the study. All frames were enlarged to 8 by 10 in. so precise reading of all relationships could be made.

Data broke down in two basic categories of readable evidence: the flow of interaction, day-by-day and hour-by-hour, as seen in the hospital lunchroom; and the exact seating of individuals day-by-day throughout the week. This latter evidence was the most significant in the study for it showed that social structure was created by the technological structure and there was little visiting between specialties in this free period. There was no apparent racial segregation within the going structure. Negroes sat with specialists of the same professional level—doctors sat with doctors, whether they were Negro or white. On the other hand, the study showed considerable range in the proportion of Negroes and other non-Caucasian groups in different departments—an imbalance of actual roles comparable to and reflecting the levels of real opportunity in the larger society.

The spontaneous nature of the circumstance chosen for tracking and counting operated as a control over what the hospital public relations officer might tell the outsider looking into hospital culture. Indeed, the empirical nature of the evidence would have qualified data gathered by individual interviewing, if the design of the research had included such an investigation. This was an observation of social structure in motion studied by direct photographic observation.

Observation of school culture in San Francisco presented a similar problem for Alyce Cathey, a teacher in a racially diverse grade school (1964). The formal culture of the classroom was another facade across the real social structure and personal interaction of her pupils. To deepen her understanding of her students' problems, Miss Cathey went to the school yard in order to view the spontaneous regrouping of her children's social life. In this case it was the institutionalized social behavior compared to the dominating peer group culture that took over as soon as the students left the classroom.

Before she could analyze the culture of her pupils, Alyce Cathey, like Rotman, needed a large pool of empirical data of *what really happened in the yard.* Noontime in the school yard offered her the same sort of opportunity as the lunch hour in the hospital. For two weeks Miss Cathey made sweeping, as well as detailed, studies of her students eating lunch and playing games in the school yard. Her role as a teacher allowed her to circulate around the grounds and photograph without causing social disruption, and she was able to get a repetitive sample of her children's world in motion outside the schoolroom.

Miss Cathey studied the photographs on the 35 mm contact sheets and selected 8 by 10 in. enlargements. She used these contact sheets in her interviews with her students. The pictures clearly showed the personality roles and clique patterns within which the girls operated, and the interview statements gave insights into the students' culture and a recognition of the way they viewed themselves and each other. For example, one Negro girl from the high fifth apparently felt rejected by her predominantly Chinese classmates, and sought daily gratification by eating with the younger children of Miss Cathey's low fifth. Day after day the camera revealed her sitting on the periphery of the low fifth group. Closer study revealed a strong but covert prejudice of the Chinese toward Negro students.

The photographic study also threw light on the nutritional habits of her students. Some of the students brought large lunches which they often shared. Others brought small lunches, usually devoid of vegetables and fruits. A few individuals had money to buy chips and imitation fruit juices; this functioned as a status symbol for the more affluent children. All but one brought their food in paper bags; this girl brought her lunch in a tin box, saying, "My mother feels paper bags for lunch are wasteful and you can't carry tea to drink in a paper bag." She was from an orthodox Chinese home where tea was considered an essential.

An added research value of a photographic tracking study such as this is that the examination can be repeated next year or the year after that to evaluate any evolution of school culture in this multi-ethnic neighborhood.

Observations of Micro-Culture

Observing how people mingle and regroup themselves is basic to an understanding of social structure in motion. Psychologically and socially, photographs diagram spatial relationships of gatherings. What are the cluster patterns? Do they represent a focal point of leadership?

In the dynamics of micro-culture, the details of person-to-person relationships can be analyzed through the use of still pictures. Photographs allow for the observation of personal physical bearing, posture, facial expressions, arm and hand gestures. Birdwhistell has developed methods for decoding this visual language of "kinesics" (1952). Hall has studied the significance of what he calls "proxemics," such things as the spacing between people and body orientation, which vary from culture to culture and according to circumstances (1966). Space can tell us much about how people communicate within their cultures. How close, how much touching, when they talk to one another? Is there a formality of space, a ring of privacy that is not open to the public? Space around and between people may reflect perception of inferiority or superiority, may single out the outcast or the deviant. Each culture has definite established modes for handling space.

An understanding of such tangibles in group behavior allowed Paul Byers to abstract from photographs certain basic patterns of group dynamics observed at a conference of American and foreign Fulbright Scholars meeting at an American college. By close analysis of just nine of these photographs Byers was able to demonstrate radically changing yet predictably patterned behavior as the circumstances of the conference progressed. His reading of three of these will give an idea of the sort of behavior that was objectively photographed for analysis.

The first example shows the scholars at a reception in the lounge. Behavior is structured consistently around the event of initial polite interaction. Byers observes:

> The group is dispersed fairly evenly in the room. The space is filled fairly evenly throughout. The furniture is also dispersed evenly throughout the room. All suit jackets are kept on and everyone wears his name tag.
>
> People sit with a fairly uniform space between themselves and tend to sit at the front edge of the chairs and sofas (except in the bucket-type chairs in which this is almost impossible). Coffee cups are uniformly placed in relation to the edges of tables. Although there is uniformity of coffee-cup placement on each table, the two tables are different from each other [at the edge on one table and about two inches from the edge on the other].
>
> Backs are generally straight, with people leaning towards each other from the waist and inclining their heads toward each other.
>
> There is little leg-crossing and no visible crossing of arms across chests.
>
> There is a repeated male position of legs apart with forearms resting just behind knees and hands together (and visible) in front.
>
> People are most commonly talking in twos—sometimes threes.
>
> Almost everyone is in eye-to-eye contact with another person and every person exhibits at least some body-orientation toward the person to whom he is talking.
>
> No two or more people in direct communication have furniture between them (Mead and Byers, 1967).

The second photograph was taken on the evening of the second day of the conference during a free time period. Here group behavior is in contrast to the first record above. Circumstances have altered the character of group patterns completely. People seem acquainted as suggested by freer expressions, closer body proximity.

> No one is seen wearing a suit-jacket but two have been brought.
>
> The commonest sitting position is forward on the chairs or sofas with bodies leaning toward others. Men's arms again tend to be resting on legs.
>
> There are more people in less space than in the earlier scene. Space between people is less and there is some body contact.
>
> Furniture has been moved to form a kind of circle and people are interacting both one-to-one and across the circle (Mead and Byers 1967).

Byers points out that it is significant that the room was dimly lit, and hypothesizes that "all other things being equal, people will change the nature of their facial expressions, will interact with their faces closer together, and/or will increase their speech articulation when low illumination decreases the clear sharp visibility among themselves" (Mead and Byers 1967).

Byers goes on to describe other meetings, most of them conforming to one of three basic patterns of relationships: the one-to-one, the many-to-one represented by audience and speaker or performer, and the circle—a leaderless equi-distance

group in which any member may in turn command attention in a one-to-many relationship. These patterns are all so familiar as to seem only of theoretical
significance; they represent culturally regulated behavior that we as Americans have
always taken for granted. But would these scholars have performed in the same way
within the context of an Arabian University with Arabian hosts?

Byers' ninth photograph illustrates the point that patterns in other cultures
may be very different. This scene shows a group of scholars, only one of them an
American, sitting on the grass in a self-limited space within touching distance of
each other. But body positions conform to no regular pattern. Byers reports that
most Americans studying the picture assume the group is listening to a concert or
a lecture outside the scope of the photograph—which was not the case. This is the
only reasonable explanation for an American. But the group is primarily not American. They may be meditating, relaxed and unconcerned, not compelled to relate in
an American way to those next to them. A group of Navajos in similar positions
could be having a political discussion. Byers demonstrates that "group" implies the
participation by its members in shared and observable regularities of behavior.
The pattern of these behaviors varies considerably, but always within a range which
is culturally narrow and specific and can be accounted for by factors in the context.

The small interrelated community is often baffling because of its very fluid
nature. This can be particularly true in communities undergoing rapid change where
the reality of social structure is likely to be found in this regrouping process. The
first look at a historically oriented community can be deceptive. Leaders may wish to
keep the image of traditional culture alive and may be eager to give the impression
that the social structure is based on historical background, with old families whose
forefathers settled the region identified as the first families—the status group that
holds the power and gets things done. Stimulated by this lead we are tempted to
cast personalities in this descending order: old families, owners of factories and
large land holdings, down through an anonymous middle class, to laborers and industrial workers. This endowed order may have been real a few decades ago, but
under the impact of economic change, with opportunities for rapidly shifting social
positions, this classic structure can be misleading, for it tells us nothing about the
fluid nature of society or the present real power divisions. The conventional view
also tells us nothing about where actual personalities fit into the structure. Such diagrams can remain empty boxes until we can fill them in with the real functions of
individuals.

In the traditional community we are confronted with the problem of the
ideal, as compared to the realistic function of community, the first with its roots in
history and the second based on rapid change and opportunism within which the
pragmatic developments of a town take place. In a sense, these are the overt and
covert scenes of human relations, where ceremonial decisions are made at the Episco-
pal Church, for example, and other formal gatherings of the town, but significant
deals are made under the table.

How can we distinguish the functioning real from the traditional ideal?
This was one of the problems confronting a fieldworker on a community study project in Canada. He suspected that he had been seeing only the facade of the social
structure. A unique social occasion presented itself where the less formally struc-

tured functioning of the community might be observed. This was the opening dance of the local yacht club which had traditionally been a high status occasion in the social life of the town. He had reason to believe that a new aggressive crowd had taken over the yacht club, and this occasion, which was not open to the general public, might indicate how social structure in the town was bending. As project photographer, I offered to photograph this opening event, an invitation that was accepted with a sense of fun by the club officers. But what would the guests and members feel when the fieldworker and I appeared with flash bulbs and cameras? In the spirit of the gay party circumstance, or because of it, the photography was greeted hilariously and we were able to record uninterruptedly throughout the evening who danced with whom, who embraced whom, who flirted with whom, who withdrew in confidential talk. The interaction observed was a scramble of the conventionally presented image of this town's social structure. Old status mingled significantly with new power groups in the seclusion of the club. There was considerable drinking despite the traditionally dry sentiments of the community, where drinking in public was taboo.

We rapidly made enlargements of representative scenes of the evening showing all the participants of the event. The fieldworker, to his delight, found that everyone involved wanted to look over and talk about the yacht club pictures. The research result of this feedback was that complete identification of all personalities was made, and with the aid of tracing paper overlays it was possible to make sociograms of complex interaction representing one real view of the social structure and interaction.

The cluster patterns between various individuals did suggest a shifting power structure. In this confidential circumstance historical leaders were seen paying court to lower status business operators who were indeed taking over the effective leadership of the community. Interview responses pointed out the covert nature of this interaction. Mr. So-and-So would never be sitting next to Mr. X, except at the yacht club party. Mrs. Z. would never be seen dancing with Mr. Y. except on this occasion. In a sense, the yacht club party was a projection of covert social structure that might become the acknowledged structure in another decade. One of the rich returns of this experiment was the significant measure of spatial position which could be compared to the formal social positions of public life—the latter creating the facade of historical social structure. Sociometric tracking often offers us this opportunity of precise measuring and comparison of social interaction. (See also discussion of projective interviewing, Chap. 6.)

Risks to Rapport in Photographic Probing

Photography can gain us a foothold in a community. But just as fast, and completely, photography can get us rejected if we are guilty of insensitive intrusion with the camera. It must be clear that when we start photographing the inner workings of social structure (as opposed to its outer institutionalized form) we leave the public domain and enter the confines of more private belief and behavior.

Cultural activities encircle a community, from the outer, impersonal, and wholly open functions taking place in the public domain, to very personal and guarded activities of families and individuals. We may photograph freely in the outer rings of public gatherings and basic technologies, but as we move inward the ground becomes more treacherous, and we should accept the fact that there may be inner sanctums we never will be able to observe with the camera. We have these circumstances within our own culture, where photographing may be completely unacceptable, extremely dangerous or literally impossible.

In many cultures, religious worship is one of the delicate function of a community. The church, the temple, the Indian kiva, are places where the deepest values are experienced. These sites and circumstances are steeped in protocol and are hypersensitive to strangers and lack of respect. In many societies this sensitivity also involves covert or outspoken fears of magic danger.

Most Indian pueblos of the American Southwest prohibit photography of ceremonial dances. In Santo Domingo, koshares, the dancing clown-priests, will grab a tourist's camera, and without breaking the dancing rhythm adroitly remove the film, expose it gracefully to the light, and return it to the photographer. Isolated Indian communities in the Oaxaca region of Mexico are so suspicious of "gringo" observers that some villages forbid photography altogether. In most indigenous cultures there are objects and locations that must not be seen by the camera.

Usually religious ceremony is a focus of prestige in a culture. It frequently involves important leaders, cloaked in social roles of caste and class. Each culture presents a way in which you can ingratiate yourself to religious leaders and achieve a role that does not dishonor the ceremony. Beyond specific refinements, the approach must match dignity with dignity and respect with respect. You need not go among the Hopis to come upon this problem. You can experience it completely when you ask to photograph a friend's wedding or a service in the local synagogue.

I had just such a challenge in photographing the Amish farmers of Lancaster County, Pennsylvania, for the U.S. Department of Agriculture. Photography was met with great hostility, yet it was important to complete this study. I called on the local Amish bishop, an impressive farmer of great age. I explained my problem, outlined the worthy and honoring nature of my study which was to record the richest culture of farming in America, as a record for history and research. The bishop was hospitable but adamant. "Don't misunderstand, son. We are not unfriendly to your work. It is just that we cannot help you make graven images of men—a sin against God. But it is obvious you are already lost with that camera machine, so we don't worry about your soul. Go right ahead, son. But when we see you we will duck!"

Unquestionably the bishop told his flock who I was and what I was doing. I found the Amish cordial, but they always ducked! With this understanding I photographed agricultural techniques and social interaction as well. When my camera was down, they smiled; when I raised my camera, if they saw me they turned their backs.

This problem of rapport can be examined on two levels—research in the public domain and photography of private sanctum. There are in each culture activities open to the general public and life circumstances that are considered completely personal. When a situation ceases to be public is a culturally determined circumstance. What you can do with a camera twenty feet from a man and what you can do five feet from a man can change dramatically from culture to culture. Each culture sets its distance. We can refer to Edward T. Hall's study, *The Hidden Dimension* (1966), for a discussion of cultural distinctions in the use of space. Latin Americans often feel the need for touching, in order to talk. North Americans on the other hand usually find touching repulsive, except on very intimate terms, and then cross sexually. Moving in on people with a camera is subject to these same sensitivities.

A seasoned fieldworker might question the feasibility of our suggestion that a newcomer could stand in front of a church and make a record of everyone entering or leaving. Certainly, if you went about this in an aggressive mechanical way, it is likely that you would be stopped. On the other hand churches are prestige sites in most communities. Natives are proud of these structures; they represent the kind of locale where natives would expect you to take a picture if you were a tourist. In a small community when services end there is a spontaneous gathering as folks leave the church. A couple of shots of the church which would include the congregation would be all you would need for a spot sample of which group supports the church.

On the other hand, if you are recording who goes into bars, this is an entirely different matter. Studies of this kind have to be very sweeping street views that include the doorway of the bars, or the shots might have to be made on particular nights, when lots of people are on the streets, so that frequenters of the bars would be only one part of the sample. The key lies in whether or not the camera is felt to be a threat; a threat can be counted upon to arouse hostility.

What is public, what is personal, and what is threatening become acutely important when we consider the feedback of pictures of community interaction. Errors in taste as to what photographs you show to whom can cause more explosions than any other failure of protocol in the community study.

A critical example of improper feedback was the interview use of the photographs of the yacht club party which so aptly illustrated class structure. As described, to gain insights into interpersonal relations the fieldworker had to work with a native picture reader to cross-check the identification and position of participants at the yacht club dance. To his satisfaction, he had no problem obtaining rewarding interviews based on the photographs. In fact he was swamped with invitations, "Come and bring the yacht club photographs." Everyone in town wanted to see the pictures of this reportedly wild party. Then quite suddenly the flood of cordiality was turned to hostility, and the fieldworker and I as project photographer were bitterly criticized. We rapidly lost our investment of good will. It was clear we had made a blunder. Our mistake was obvious, for projective use of the party pictures had aided and abetted the most malicious gossips in the community. It had been an unfortunate tactical error to show *any* of these photographs to the public. Probably the set as a whole should have been shown only to our one trusted key informant, who in the end gave us the most complete reading of the event.

This experience suggests a safe rule-of-thumb protocol. Pictures made in the public domain can be fed back into the public domain. Pictures made in private circumstances should be shown *only to people in these circumstances*. Pictures of a family can with gratification be fed back to the family, but should never be shown to other families no matter how good friends. A possible exception would be more or less formal portraits taken to represent the accepted public image.

In general, photographic notes should be handled in the same way as other field notes. Material given in confidence should be held in confidence, and for a family to let you record their private life is an act of the greatest confidence.

Considering the retention of the subjects' good feeling as an integral part of ethical research procedure the anthropologist will, of course, pursue his research objectives with honor and discretion. We feel that one professional accomplishment of the fieldworker is to leave with the door open behind him, so that he can return with welcome as many times as may be necessary to complete his study. Generally, the success of field study is dependent upon the generosity of the native culture.

On one occasion I had the assignment of recording a Navajo sandpainting, but Navajo singers offered no cooperation to a white man with a camera. Trader Roman Hubbell of Ganado was amazed and amused at what I considered a dilemma. "Why don't you buy a ceremony? That's what a Navajo would do. Who have you been approaching? After all, you wouldn't expect one of your white friends to share his medical treatment with you." The solution was as simple as stated. We had no difficulty buying a sandpainting of our own, and once the deal was made, fear of magic dangers dwindled amazingly. With complete cooperation we photographed each step of the ceremony, and were invited to record in detail the contents of the singer's medicine bundle. Most of the time there is a gracious way of carrying out your documentation.

6

Interviewing with Photographs

W HAT IS THE VALUE of interviewing with photographs? There is the unique return of insights that might be impossible to obtain by other techniques, but there is also photography's support of interviewing in general. A brief review of the challenges of this basic methodology will show us where and how questioning the native with photographs can help us gather data and enhance our understanding.

A first and basic hurdle to interviewing is getting inside the native's house. This involves presenting reasons for calling. It requires introducing your role, explaining your purpose in asking questions, and touching upon the focus of your research. To be sure, sometimes you can obscure both role and purpose, and interview only by skillful and friendly conversation. But in extended community research this is hardly practical, as everyone knows something about you anyway: "You're one of those fellows from the city university who is asking all sorts of questions for some sort of a study."

Once you make contact, the problem is to hold on to this circumstance and in some way make the native like your visits. If he asks you to stay on and have a piece of cake and a cup of coffee, you feel you have made it. Maybe he will open the door for a second interview. Then the problem arises that usually in the first evening the farmer has given out all his knowledge, or at least thinks he has, and is bewildered that you suggest a second interview. Even when genuinely welcoming you back, the farmer may flinch when you begin to question him. "I told you all about that last time." Sometimes he gets surly and you've had your last interview.

Of course you fend against the human relations stumbling blocks whatever they may be. You may think of favors you can do for the informant or of little gifts that can be brought as appetizers. You struggle to share some genuine function with this farmer or craftsman, so that you can gain acceptance and view the culture from within.

If all the basic human challenges are mastered, the problem is to get the level and kind of data the research needs. Of course, effective interviewing techniques vary considerably depending upon the size and nature of the project, the

46

group or culture being studied, the pressure of time, and the breadth or narrowness of the probing. But generally a good interview is not just a lot of good-natured meandering talk, but real insight into subjects which may be highly specialized. Sometimes the informant is *too* loquacious, will not stop for a question, just winds on all evening about trivia. This situation is difficult if you expect to transcribe every utterance of the evening. On the other hand, if you are too blunt and structured in your probing, he may give perfunctory answers, or just shut up. You want deep feelings, you want strong values and expressive imagery, but unless you are making strictly open-ended non-directive interviews you seek expressions in your prescribed area, such as the problems of technological change. Often your informant will be politely cautious and keep the interview on a formal or superficial level, no strong stands or feelings, and you get only a shallow recovery. When you press for more confidence or sharper opinions, again he can become hostile, and the interview is lost.

Memory trauma is another block. Often the old man of the village "just can't recall" and goes around in circles. A problem met in cross-cultural interviewing is the limitation and confusion of verbal meaning. This can keep your notes on a very shallow or very unreliable level.

A final problem is recording. How good a memory have you for exact names and details? Sometimes when you bring out a notebook, the interview goes cold. (Using a tape-recorder is a very specialized technique, perhaps as complicated as photography, though some investigations need verbatim recording.)

How Photographs Function in Interviewing

The first tempting use of photographs in interviewing has already been sketched—photograph taking can itself establish your entree to the interview. The spontaneous anticipation of feedback, the excitement of seeing images of self and a mirrored view of the environment, rarely fails to get an invitation to come and show the photographs. Images of the familiar are compelling, and if only to see the records you are welcome in the native's house, at least in cultural areas where the process is understood and accepted. Returning photographs to native collaborators makes a functional reason for calling. Only a few doors will not be opened expectantly with this introduction.

Once inside the house, the photographs make directional conversation pieces that allow you to draw out the interests and enthusiasms of your informant. The theme of the interview is nonverbally established, and because this photographic feedback creates a state of awareness and evokes emotional feelings, the photographs make wordless probes that lead the interview into the heart of your research.

In the Stirling County Study (Collier 1957) and later on the Navajo Reservation, we made tests to compare interviewing with photographs to interviewing with strictly verbal probes. In both tests the pattern that emerged was that the cycle of verbal interviewing went from good to poor, and second and third interviews were difficult and sometimes impossible to make. Interviews with photographs retained the same level of return from the first to the third visit. Explanation given by the fieldworkers in Canada was that isolated country people said all there was to say in the initial interview and the succeeding interviews tended to become purely social. Often with the Navajos and to some extent with the Canadian workers, intensive probing for structured information made the informants uneasy or even angry. On the other hand the photographs gave them something to talk about, which made structured questioning less of a strain.

Photographs sharpen the memory and give the interview an immediate character. The informant is back on his fishing vessel, working out in the woods, or carrying through a skillful craft. The projective opportunity of the photographs offers a gratifying sense of self-expression as the informant is able to explain and identify content and educate the interviewer with his wisdom.

Skillfully presented photographs divert the informant from wandering out of the research area. Without verbal pressure, another photograph drawn from your briefcase will bring the conversation back into the field of study. Photo-interviewing allows for very structured conversation without any of the inhibitive effect of questionnaires or compulsive verbal probes.

Projective material in the interview functions as a third agent. Photographs, examined by the anthropologist and the native together, become the object of discussion. This appears to reduce stress in the interview by relieving the informant of being the *subject* of the interrogation. Instead his role can be one of the expert guide leading the fieldworker through the content of the pictures. The photographs allow him to tell his own story spontaneously. This usually elicits a flow of information about personalities, places, processes, and artifacts. The facts are in the pictures, the informant does not have to feel he is divulging confidences. All he is doing is getting the history in order and the names straight. This objectivity allows and invites the use of a notebook or even a tape-recorder. "You better get these names straight!" For the anthroplogist is making notes *about the photographs,* so it appears, not writing down incriminating judgments about the informant's life (though often the hypnotic pull of the photographs does make him reveal very great confidences). Photographic interviewing offers a detachment that allows the maximum free association possible within structured interviewing.

How long can we extend these examinations? The interview visit commonly offers you new opportunities for photography. "I would like to come on Sunday and make portraits of your family." A second acting out interview opens the door for another projective interview, and it is possible to continue interviewing indefinitely as long as the photographic process continues. Your second and third interviews can be as intense as your first, a rather rare accomplishment in strictly verbal querying.

The Photo-Essay Approach to Photo-Interviewing

In the chapters on photographing technology and social interaction, I have touched on the most common return of photo-interviewing, the gleaning of cyclopedic information. Interviewing with photographs of housing surveys, records of technologies and public circumstances of interaction give valuable and complete factual insights and identifications. I have tried to stress the fact that relatively simple photography *can* yield important data. The box camera is capable of distinguishing houses and counting the number of cars and people on Main Street. The functions of counting, measuring, and identifying that have proven to be scientifically reliable depend on relatively simple elements that any novice with the camera can record.

But below this surface content, so valuable in the orientation phase of a community study, photographs are charged with psychological and highly emotional elements and symbols. In a depth study of culture it is often this very fact that allows the native reader to express his ethos. *Methodologically, the only way we can use the full record of the camera is through the projective interpretation by the native.*

When we consider the intensity of people's response to pictures of themselves we raise the question—Can any photograph offer this? This query implies another —How good must the ethnographic camera record be to allow for significant research interpretation? As we move from factual to projective reading of photographs by natives, we must be concerned with the complete content of *all* the emotional and evocative elements that can be documented by the camera. Reasonably, the richer the photographs the more intense the potential projective response.

Methodologically, the challenge of comprehensive evaluation of life experience suggests the photo-essay as an approach to anthropological description using every sense and skill of the photographer-observer. When we assemble a photo-interview kit to probe Navajo life values we are in effect presenting a selected essay on Navajo life which we have gathered and designed to give the Indian informant an opportunity to speak of the values and subtleties of his culture. The selection, stimuli, and language facility of the imagery determine the success of the venture. These are also the key elements in the reportage of the photo-essay.

The technique of photo interpretation by the subject of the photograph allows the ethnographic photographer to record and follow through scientifically themes such as the passage of a man through his culture, as Redfield suggests. When the photographic essay has been read by the native, it can become a meaningful and authentic part of the anthropologist's field notes, for when interview responses are studied against these projective photographs, overtones and circumstantial detail can be reevaluated and the full richness of photographic content can find a place in the data and literature of anthropology.

We turn to a community regional study for an example of how an intense level of photography and projective interviewing can support anthropology. This example is part of an experimental test of photo-interviewing described in full in an article in the *American Anthropologist* (Collier 1957).

The Stirling County Study of the Maritimes of Canada was particularly concerned with migration caused by technological and economic change, which appeared to be a major variable in the mental health of the region. Acadian farmers were moving into the English industrial town of Bristol to find wage work in fish plants and lumber mills. This movement raised many questions on how the migration was taking place. Some Acadians sold out and moved permanently into the English industrial center, but there also appeared a gradual movement up the coast from the provincial heart of the French-speaking population. Acadians had bought farms on the periphery of the predominantly English area where they remained as part-time farmers and commuted to the mills each day to work. Were these French going to give up their farming and become urban dwellers? Or was the pull of culture going to keep them on the soil? Was there a notable shift to English values? Or were the Acadians remaining French with strong ties in their traditional settlements? Was this migration stressful? Did the Acadians like working in industries owned and run by the English? Was life in the urban English center satisfying?

Interviewing was the methodology at this phase of the community study, and to gain further insights a projective photo-interview study was considered. As soon as I began assembling the interview material the character of the photographic research changed. I was no longer just making a survey which involved precise selection and documentation. Instead I was realistically involved in a photographic essay, shooting and selecting elements that were to give a comprehensive overlook in a limited number of enlarged 8-by-10-in. prints. Through the use of these prints the interviewer and I hoped to evoke responses that would give us an inside look into this contemporary Acadian cultural problem.

The design for this project required several separate studies: (1) industrial life in the English center; (2) photo-essay on the family; (3) a housing survey of the immediate area; (4) samples of public interaction in nearby towns.

This pool of material was to probe: (1) Were Acadian migrants happy doing industrial work in the English town? (2) Was the belt between the Acadian and English areas clearly one of migration and transition? (3) Were the Acadians here going to remain French and part-time farmers, or were they in the process of shifting to an Anglo industrial workers' culture.

The Plenns, one of the families contacted for this study, lived on a farm in the presumed migratory belt and both husband and wife worked in a lumber-processing plant in Bristol. The first subject of field photography was this lumber and box mill. I photographed long views showing the mill and the town of Bristol. I documented the man and wife at their various jobs, and the interior of the mill in general. After quitting time I made records of Bristol's shopping center showing the stores and throngs of people on the streets.

A date was set to call on our family with the first feedback. The mill pictures showed a most dangerous industrial interior, and we expected that they would tell us in no uncertain terms that they disliked their jobs.

George Plenn and his wife, Violet, met us cordially at the door of their neat two-story farmhouse and ushered us into the dining room. The anthropologist-interviewer got out his notebook, and we proceeded to examine the photographs. The Plenns looked at each picture with great interest and gave very complete and detailed information. But we were completely mistaken in predicting an emotionally charged expression about life in the mill. They were equally noncommittal on the views of the streets of Bristol. They recognized no people and scarcely knew the names of any stores. Finally the wife explained, "When we are through work we are sick of Bristol and want to come right home. . . . When we want something during the week we buy it at the corner store, and on Saturday night we always do our shopping in Portsmouth," (a town on the edge of the Acadian half of the county, in the opposite direction from Bristol). Though we were disappointed about not getting one emotional statement about the industrial environment, the responses to the photographs were significantly revealing. The couple was not involved with the town of Bristol. They knew no one on the streets and all their commercial life was south in the nearest French-oriented community. They went to Bristol to make cash wages, and talked about the mill as, "a fine place to work . . . good pay . . . good job," and seemed to have a cultivated lack of concern for the questionable safety or the haphazard working conditions.

For the second photographic coverage we spent a day on the Plenns' farm. My wife, Mary Trumbull Collier, and I and our two-year-old son arrived at the farm on a Saturday afternoon just as the family was driving up after a half day's work. My purpose was to gather material for an interview on home values and the rewards of living on a farm. This was definitely not a survey, but rather an acted-out interview and a photographic essay on the family. It was also an example of participant observation requiring considerable mutual satisfaction. We had to be totally at ease and enjoying ourselves and they in return had to be gratified and humanly rewarded for their hospitality and communication.

It is awkward and sometimes impossible to stand back aloofly while making human records. No type of fieldwork requires better rapport than an intimate photographic account of family culture. Yet in another way, spending a photographic day with a family can be less intruding than the same hours spent asking and answering endless verbal questions. As with the observing photographer on the fishing boat, the intrusion is *visual* not *verbal*. The native does not have the stress of constant explanation, or anxiety over what you are doing standing by silently. The photographer is as active as the busy fisherman or farmer. The presence of my wife and young son added further human trust to a circumstance that might have been tense. My wife was in the house sharing canning techniques with Violet Plenn while I was accompanying Mr. Plenn on his chores.

After a period of tensions as everyone got used to the routine of photography, members of the family began responding creatively to the opportunity of recording. They spontaneously began acting out elements of their lives that were particularly gratifying or significant. Pets, favorite hens, ducks, special skills were called to the attention of the camera. There was plenty of talk, but it was not an interview; it was mutual communication in which we returned as much as we were given. The afternoon was climaxed with an excellent meal and we parted feeling fast friends.

Our second interview was markedly different from the first. We were met at the door with great expectation, and fairly dragged into the dining room to show the family pictures. The Plenns looked through the home studies with great intensity. They interjected their comments on the farm pictures with the heated statements about the mill in Bristol we had expected them to make on our first visit. It occurred to us that maybe they had never really seen the mill before they examined our interview pictures, and so were unprepared to make comments. But during the period between interviews they had been considering and discussing the mill. Our pictures may have upset them very much. And as they viewed their vegetable garden they commented on how sad life must be in Bristol for Acadians who had given up their farms. "There wouldn't be anything to do after work but sleep." They were vehement that they would never leave their farm and move to Bristol. Our projective examination had thus far given us many answers as to how the Plenns felt about migration to Bristol.

The third set of photographs was a series of surveys: the houses scattered along the road of the Plenns' community in the heart of the zone between the Acadian and the English areas; a religious festival at the Catholic Church in Plenns' parish; and the Plenns shopping in the crowded Acadian-English community of Portsmouth on Saturday evening. Our research goal in this final interview was to get, if possible, the names and backgrounds of all the people living along the mile of road in the Plenns' community, and to test the Plenns on their knowledge of Portsmouth. Were they really as involved in this center as they claimed they were? The religious picnic, we hoped, would indicate the degree of Acadian culture in this supposedly transitional area.

The third and final interview was the most exhausting for the Plenns and the note-taking anthropologist. The pictures were highly readable and the data poured out as fast as they could read the pictures. The family went down the road, house for house, describing in a structured way who the people were—if they were Acadian or English, and how long they had lived in the area. Only one house bogged down the pace of their reading. This house picture was looked at and passed over with smiles and shrugs. "Who lives here?" More smirks. "Just an old woman." "What does she do? Farm? Have a pension?" "She don't do nothing." "We don't know nothing about her." We passed on to the next house and continued on our routine interrogation. Obviously they did know about the woman, but because the house was surely the scene of questionable or deviant behavior, they did not care to discuss it. Invariably photographs will unearth this kind of emotional censorship.

It was very clear that Plenns' area was not a migration belt as such. People had owned homes here for generations. The church festival showed many Acadian people, but they were identified as coming from elsewhere in the French speaking area.

It was late, and the interview had run beyond the point of productive return when we studied the Portsmouth shopping pictures. Still the Plenns were able to identify almost everyone on the street, tell where they came from, even when a back was turned or when the person was standing a block away.

This is typical of the sharp recognition of rural people, whether they be farmers in Kansas or forest laborers in Canada. Photo-interviewing offers the anthropologist a key to this native knowledge. For the same reason, photo-reading can be a check on native familiarity. "Yeah, I know all the folks up there in Prairie Corners." But show your informant photographs of interaction in this community, and you will know just how much your native really knows about this settlement— many people, a few people, or no people. This check is equally clear in areas of technology and geography. It is easy to recognize when a man is out of his field.

Our pictures of the streets of Bristol, the Plenns' home community, and shopping in Portsmouth adequately tracked this family's geographic movements. A straight line to the mill and home, another line to Portsmouth to trade, and a very long line back to Plenn's traditional home in the Acadian part of the county. Plenn's English-Protestant wife seemed to have joined his social culture completely, for all their interaction took place to the south with his relatives; none took place to the north in Bristol.

It is methodologically important to note that our sessions with the Plenns were *group interviews*. Violet Plenn's eighteen-year-old daughter and an eight-year-old adopted boy, as well as Violet and George, all looked at the pictures together, handing them around a circle. This affected the quality of responses, possibly inhibiting emotional association and encouraging more factual responses. In the deeper probing about life in Bristol we may have lost data. But in the identification of the housing survey and social interaction in Portsmouth we gained data manyfold. Group interviewing with photographs can become a game, each member competing against the group to give the most comprehensive information. A group interview situation without graphic probes too frequently becomes nondirectional parlor talk.

We have described two very contrasting types of recording—the intensely personal photo-essay analysis of culture, and the impersonal documenting of community structure and interaction. Both approaches yielded valuable data, and our study could not have been completed without the support of both approaches. But the family essay brought insights that were more subtle and usually more difficult to recover, the heartfelt sentiments about migration into the English industrial center and, in the face of industrial wage work, the persistent fulfilling need of owning a farm. These sentiments were a projective response to the feedback which compared their ideal life to the driving, industrial life in Bristol. These opposites would not have been clearly realized in the feedback of the Plenns' life without the support of photographic content.

Photo-Interviewing in Preliterate Cultures

"Many indigenous and nonliterate peoples have had no experience with photographs. They do not think in two dimensional images. You cannot count on your photo-interviewing technique except with those who are well westernized." This is an opinion I have heard expressed by a number of colleagues. If this were true a major application of photographic research would be lost to anthropology. But was it true? Much scientific tradition suggested it might be, though it had never been put to systematic test.

My first opportunity to seek an answer in an indigenous society was presented in Cornell's Fruitland Project with the Navajo Indians of New Mexico. Again, I was part of a community study, a development program among Indians who had recently been relocated as agriculturists. The Indians were undergoing further rapid social change because the adjoining area was suddenly becoming industrialized because of the development of natural gas. Many of the Navajos were only part-time farmers, making wages laying oil lines and working in gas plants. To be sure this was no primitive unexposed tribe in the Highlands of New Guinea, but the group as a whole was sufficiently unacculturated to make our observations of their perceptual processes significant.

Since the focus of the study was the changing attitudes of Navajo life values, I assembled 20 photographs of typical Navajo circumstances. Most of the pictures had been taken on other parts of the reservation. We did not want to confuse our results by the conventional reluctance of Navajos to talk about familiar persons or familiar settings; this was bad taste and could be charged as witchcraft. The selection, which we planned to use as probes to get expressions of contemporary value, covered sheep culture, weaving arts, food, agriculture and family life. William A. Ross, then a graduate student at University of Arizona, was assigned the job of interviewing.

After the first round of interviews, we had our initial answer: there was no doubt at all that the Navajos could interpret two dimensional images. The truth was that they interpreted photographs much more specifically than the farmers and fishermen in Canada. Like the Spindlers working with the Blood Indians (see page 61), we received little projective material, no stories about the universe or the future of the Navajo people. We were given instead exact detailed accounts of what was happening in each scene.

The Navajos read photographs as literally as we urban Westerners read books or mariners read charts. A typical example: We handed a panoramic view to Hosteen Greyhills, a Navajo farmer. He held the photograph firmly with both hands, studied it with some apparent confusion, then began moving in a circle, till finally his face lit up. "That's how he was standing. There is the East. Sun has just risen, it's early in the morning. The picture is in the spring, it was made at Many Farms the first year of farming." The picture was laid down emphatically. "How do you know it is Many Farms?" Greyhills raised the picture again with some irritation, "See . . . those head gates. Nowhere else do they have head gates like that. See . . . it's the stubble of the first cover crop. No hogans. People living over there." He gesticulated out of the picture. "Spring—nothing growing." The picture was laid down for good and a second photograph was studied. Greyhills' analysis of the panorama seemed uncanny. With a magnifying glass shapes could be made out that might be head gates. There certainly were no hogans. To our amateur eyes the cover crop was unrecognizable. But the reading was 100 percent correct. The photograph had been made five years earlier, at Many Farms, 80 miles to the southwest in the first year of this agricultural project from a mesa looking over the valley at perhaps 7:30 in the morning.

We were dealing with a phenomenon having nothing to do with modern acculturation—exposure to movies and weekly reading of *Life* magazine—but with the sensory perception of a preliterate culture in which a man must survive by astute visual analysis of the clues of his total ecology. Hosteen Greyhills was applying to our photographs the same level of visual perception and fluency he would apply as he stepped out of his hogan to look around the horizon for his grazing horse. We surmised that people living close to nature have to be specialists in natural phenomena to survive. Hence, Navajos read our photographs in the same way, reading each common clue, and coming to a shared consensus of what was happening. The Western observer in urban culture is usually a specialist in a single field. Outside this area, modern urban man tends to be visually illiterate.

We handed Greyhills a photograph of a handsome Navajo couple playing with a baby on a cradle board, and expected information on child rearing and family relations, but instead: "That boy has been away to school. He has come back, and

A theme of culture: roast mutton! This document brought intense response in our projective examination of changing Navajo values.

he's training to be a medicine man. He's either going to a ceremony or coming from one." The picture was laid down on the ground. "But how do you know he's been away to school?" Again the exasperated grab at the photograph. "See, anyone can see he's been away to school . . . look at that hair cut. Look at those glasses. Can't you see his moccasins? His turquoise? His belt? Of course he's going to a ceremony. Too young to be a singer. Must be helper. Wants to be medicine doctor." Again the analysis was correct. The photograph had been made after a sandpainting ceremony. The young man *had* been away to school and *was* training to be a singer. We, of course, saw the moccasins and jewelery but were not sufficiently versed in contemporary Navajo patterns to realize that now moccasins are rarely worn except at ceremonies.

The result of our experiment was that the photographs were read so evenly by all our informants that the responses were similarly structured, both in content and in length. The test showed a very even containment of values. The longest responses were about sheep culture, next came weaving, and the poorest return was on the agricultural photographs. This was reasonable. Though Navajos have always done some farming, status and security have been measured in sheep. The picture that consistently drew the most enthusiastic responses, accompanied by grins and happy talk, was a close-up photograph of roast mutton!

Yet there was one photographic circumstance that had we depended on its reading, would have made us conclude that Navajos could not interpret two dimensional images. This was a very clear record of horses in the government corral in this Navajo farming community. "What is going on in this picture?" Our informants looked at the photograph in utter bewilderment as if they never had seen horses in a corral before. "We can't imagine what is happening. Maybe it's a rodeo. Maybe they are going to have a race." *No one* would interpret this photograph. Here was a scene of deepest Navajo anger and hurt, the government corral where surplus stock was held for sale or destruction to rid the range of useless overstocked herds—useless to the Soil Conservation Service, but a source of prestige and joy to the Navajos, whose status is traditionally measured in fine horses and livestock.

I had been told that the Indians in the Peruvian Andes could not interpret photographs; this was an emphatic statement by an excellent fieldworker who had worked in the Andes, and was based on a specific experience of the misreading of a photograph. Later I had the opportunity of spending a year photographing a cultural baseline for Allan R. Holmberg's Cornell-Peru Project of social and technological changes at Vicos. On the basis of my colleague's experience, we were prepared to find that these Andean Indians had difficulty reading photographs. Then one day when my wife was washing negatives in a ditch Indian children gathered around curiously, and to her amazement recognized portraits of their friends *in the negative*. Soon after that the young Indian who cooked for some of the hacienda staff recognized his house in an aerial photograph. We began to suspect that Vicosinos could read photographs as well as the Navajos.

Later in our study we informally tested the perception of the Vicos Indians. We made up a set of photographs that included Indians working in fields, scenes of weaving, views of Indian homes and a view of the central hacienda buildings. Quechua-speaking Peruvian anthropology students took them on their routine interview visits to see whether they would function as interview probes. The Peruvian students returned and with wonderment agreed that the Indians did have problems about looking at photographs. But further questioning revealed that their performance was contradictory. Yes, they could recognize acquaintances a hundred yards down the trail, they could point out in detail the technology of weaving, but they could not identify the panorama of the hacienda buildings. Their faces became blank. They didn't know where it was or what it was. On long scrutiny they finally recognized a little chapel on the far edge of the hacienda grounds, where they rested their coffins en route to the communal burial grounds.

Was the hacienda, the real instrument of their peonage, such a hateful place that they didn't even want to discuss it? Or was it so traditionally upsetting that they had in fact never looked at the hacienda buildings? Likely the block was similar in nature to that which had inhibited the Navajos from talking about the government corral. But it was clear that the Indian peons could read photographs, even in the negative, even long distance photographs, so long as the visual circumstances were such that they were willing to discuss and explain the photographic content.

The Indians of Chiapas, Mexico, read photographs with sufficient perception to allow the Harvard Project to complete regional community surveys of demography and land tenure by photographic examination. This examination is reported by George A. Collier and Evon Z. Vogt (1965). The terrain of this region, ranging from 2000 to 8000 feet, the meager trails, and the multiplicity of communities necessitated developing a rapid technique of overview. A major goal of the project was an analysis of land use patterns and the general ecology. Since aerial intelligence is highly developed, aerial mapping presented an obvious solution. Spy-in-the-sky cameras can measure space and artifacts down to six feet from elevations of seventy thousand feet. There seemed no reason why the physical patterns of culture could not be defined by a similar technique. Picture reading in Army intelligence depends on precise codification; this was an equal problem in the Chiapas community and agricultural survey. The gray scale of the black and white aerial print had to be rigorously standardized to identify the sites of various crops, natural verdure, geological structure, and the variety of Indian house types. With a reliable interpretation, aerial photographs made at standard mapping heights of ten thousand feet above the valley floors were able to yield an accurate ecological overlook of the patterns of settlement and land use.

> We have found the aerial photos most useful in ethnography when examined carefully with our Tzotzil informants, who, fascinated by this means of looking at the world, provide us with highly detailed information about their native communities. The photographs allow us to construct maps as accurately and completely as we might by surveying and sketching at a site itself with much greater expenditure of time and effort. (Collier and Vogt 1965:2)

In an effort to avoid interpersonal tension, the interviews were not made in the Indian communities represented in the photographs, but instead the Indian informants came to the project's headquarters where they were able to express themselves freely about the photographs. Only in the case of land use and agricultural problems are Indians interviewed on location.

The Indians had no significant difficulty identifying communities and discussing land use from these aerial records. With the aid of matched prints and stereoscopes, Indians were able to identify spaces and objects down to two feet, and to provide information to complete community interviews on home ownership and social structure.

The reliability of the insights gained in the pretest of the Chiapas study was comparable to the kind of data we have consistently recovered from interviewing with ground level regional and community studies: identification of village and habitation, ownership of land, explanation of technologies, accounts of history and movement of social and technological change. The rewarding accomplishment of this experiment, a departure from the conventional readings of army intelligence, agencies of land management, and special surveys carried out in photo-geology, was that Indian informants were also able to make projective observations from the aerial prints. The technique proved so practical that the Harvard group is carrying out a major investigation using these photographs in interviewing.

> Several days' work with a few selected informants allowed us, on the basis of the photo, to compile an exhaustive house by house census, to catalog land owner-ship on over 400 land plots, and to identify most of the community's sacred waterholes, mountains, caves, and cross shrines. This task on a village of 670 residents would have taken many weeks' time without the aerial photograph.
>
> But the aerial photos are more than a time-saving device. They allow us to tackle problems of a more general nature whose solution requires a *quantity* of data which we usually have had to sacrifice for quality, and a *quality* of data which traditionally we have had to sacrifice for breadth of scope. (Collier and Vogt 1965:2-3)

Can nonliterate people read photographs? Our testing of the Navajo, our more casual experience with the Andean Indians, and now the Harvard Chiapas Project of aerial photographic interviewing with the Mexican Indians gives us a hopeful view that many people of preliterate and less-developed cultures can trans-fer their native perception to the two dimensional image of a photograph.

Psychological Overtones of Visual Imagery in Projective Interviewing

Our consideration of photography in the framework of the community study now brings to mind deeper questions. Anthropology has extended its range of human study beyond the description and measurement of external structures and processes to a study of inner states and value systems. These latter concerns approach and overlap the areas of psychology and social psychiatry. How does the individual adjust to his culture? Anthropology is also increasingly being called upon to support broad humanistically motivated efforts of social change and de-velopment—action programs concerning education, health, and welfare, and efforts to minimize the dislocation involved in rapid technological and cultural change and migration. Many disciplines might be involved in these investigations; tech-niques and tests of both a cultural and psychological character are used to probe the more submerged nature of the individual and the community.

Photography has an important role in these refined understandings, both be-cause of its specificity and because of its ability to present interrelated wholes. As an example, the inclusion of photographs can make the familiar community question-naire more comprehensive and the meanings of questions more precise; the nonver-bal presentation can help to overcome problems of illiteracy and facilitate question-ing across the language barrier in cross-cultural studies. Photographs offer the thought process a fluency of imagery in the projective interview, an opportunity that has just begun to find its place in the research of psychological and anthropological understanding. What Goldschmidt and Edgerton say of drawings as an interview-ing tool is also true of photographs:

> . . . they present all elements simultaneously, without differential emphasis, while a statement is, by the nature of language, lineal. [Also] the symbolic meanings

of the artifacts are themselves significant, and . . . their significance is once removed when substituted for by verbal presentation (1961:44).

All varieties of cultural and psychological examinations which use photography exploit the stimulus of feedback. All rewards of interviewing with photographs stem from this phenomenon of the return to man of a familiar image of reality.

Art is Feedback. All forms of self-expression are varieties of feedback. One must consider the art experience as the return to man of that emotional and intellectual content which extends and sharpens his consciousness. Psychologically man cannot survive without feedback any more than he can healthfully survive without his culture. His very intelligence depends on a constant renewal of awareness, and it is through feedback in painting, balladry, story telling, and in modern man story reading and film viewing, that he acquires and retains his intelligence about himself and his life circumstance. The function of this realization process takes place equally in the objective self-expression of artistic creation and in the audience experience of absorbing feedback. Both processes create the essential state of awareness. For our thesis feedback *is* the self-realization process. Even the prisoner in the windowless cell must scratch meanings on his prison walls. Even in the darkest consciousness we must dream!

Alexander H. Leighton of Harvard University made some early explorations into the projective use of art-work which suggest the dimensions of this cultural experience. While making an anthropological study of Saint Lawrence Island in the Bering Straits, Leighton had several Eskimos draw pictures of the major events in their lives. One woman was outstanding for her capture of a whole range of human experience.

A few years later during the most volatile period of Japanese and American hostility in the Second World War, Dr. Leighton was sent for research purposes to the Japanese Relocation Center at Poston in the Mojave Desert. The conditions were unbearable and violence could be expected at any time. Dr. Leighton had a Japanese artist make literal drawings of the major stress circumstances in the camp; the result was an intensely emotional feedback in watercolors depicting the conditions in the camp in their most serious light. "All emotions entered these pictures, rage, grief, the sense of injustice, and also humor, roaring laughter, and appreciation of the desert's beauty."[1]

Byron Harvey has successfully used indigenous painting in an ethno-medical study of Hopi curing practices and ceremonies.[2] A major goal of his methodology in using Hopi artists' material in interviewing was to form a linguistic bridge so his informants could explain with cultural accuracy the beliefs and practices of native therapy. The paintings offered his informants a positive scheme which would allow for a very involved explanation using the simplest vocabulary.

A second objective was to use the painting as a lever to get into the mystique and the technology so that Harvey could ask intelligible questions. The accuracy of the paintings and Harvey's gleaned knowledge stimulated his informants to fully express knowledge that they might otherwise have glossed over.

---

[1] Private communication.
[2] Discussion at Southwestern Anthropological Association meeting at Davis, California, 1966, and private communication.

The artists selected were all painters of kachinas—ceremonial wooden dolls elaborately carved and decorated to represent supernatural forces—and sophisticated in design and color as well as informed about Hopi mysticism. These artists had no trouble in moving from abstract kachina decorations to two dimensional documentary paintings on paper. John McCaffrey, of San Francisco State College, accomplished this as easily with a native calabash bowl painter in Australia, who moved without problem from making incised images on a gourd to watercolors on 16-by-20-in. paper.[3]

While suggesting the subject, Harvey did not specifically structure the content of what the painters were to depict. "Now we are going to do a man with a broken arm." Harvey did encourage a sweep of content, to include more than one person and to show where the treatment was taking place.

Data was recovered on three levels. First, there were the revelations in the paintings themselves; second, the painter's explanation of what the records meant; and third, check interviews with ten Hopis representing various tribal clans (including three of the artists who painted the series). By including artists in this final interview series Harvey obtained a comparable level of graphic as well as cultural sophistication. This series operated informally as a control over his data and gave Harvey a rewarding parallel reading of the paintings. All interviewing was unstructured: "Here's another one." Informants gave specific information and precise linguistic identification, but also told stories and made observations about what was going on. "Sometimes we use urine to treat sore eyes." Harvey also found out that these paintings were useful in exploring where sensitive magical areas lay; in his words, "See if they dodge." Graphic interview material often reveals obvious deceptions that can form a volume of important psychological insight.

Feedback in research of this type is an effort to stimulate the native to express his multiple feelings about himself and his culture. We can feed cultural material back to the informant, allowing the native to express his life feelings, or we can get the native to express his life by manufacturing his own feedback, in paintings, drawings, story telling, or re-enacting his life for us dramatically.

John Adair of San Francisco State College and Sol Worth of the Annenberg School of Communication, University of Pennsylvania are conducting just such an experiment of dramatized feedback by having Navajo Indians make motion pictures of themselves.[4] With simple instructions in the use of a Bell and Howell three lens mount movie camera, Navajos are shooting their own films about their culture. This is an ultimate effort in projective examination allowing the native to act out his awareness of who he is and his relationship to his culture. This can then be fed back to other Navajos for further responses. The unstructured nature of such an experiment with open-ended scripting, acting, and editing might answer the important question, where a Navajo Indian is going now. Projective techniques may be the only way to capture the constantly changing mirror image of personality in a rapidly evolving modern culture.

---

[3] Private communication.
[4] Private communication.

The Position of Photographs in the
Scale of Projective Tools

When we speak of the projective use of photographs we are speaking of a distinctive experience. The Thematic Apperception Technique is one of the projective tools. Like the Rorschach cards, the TAT dredges for subjective responses. "What does this picture remind you of?" The focus is on the internal feelings and values of the informant. When we interview with photographs we can have precisely the opposite experience, for the focus is on *what is in the photographs*. Such examinations can be like a personally conducted tour through the culture *depicted in the photographs*. Realistically, the interview return is a blend of precise reading of exact graphic content and projected attitudes. In general it is this reading fluency of photographs that makes the camera record a valuable recovery tool in anthropology. Hence, we must understand that responses to paintings and drawings are on another level of projection.

A field application of both drawings and photographs used projectively clearly gives us the character of the optically produced image. George and Louise Spindler of Stanford University have experimented with both mediums while interviewing the Blood Indians of Canada with a technique called the Instrumental Activities Inventory (1963 and 1965). One question was, "Is it good to have white men's trading posts on the Blood reservation?" When they showed a *photograph* of a trading post on the reservation to an informant, the response was, "Why, that no good cheating trader McSmith! I'll never go in his post again; he's a mean, hard man." In another interview the informant was shown a *drawing* of a typical trading post, and the response this time was, "Yes, it's good to have a trading post on the reservation. Some traders can be real friends and help us Indians get the best deals. Bloods are not ready yet to run posts, and if a Blood was a trader, he'd give all the best deals to his family."[5] The Spindlers say:

> We want to avoid personalization, so that each respondent can project into the instrumental activity his own values and cognitive organization. Photographs are too specific about places, persons, and objects for our purposes. The I. A. I. (Instrumental Activities Inventory) pictures are, however, not drawn with fuzzy lines or ambiguous detail. Each item in the picture must be technically correct or the respondent becomes so concerned about the technical mistake that he fails to project much of anything but this concern. And the respondent must know what instrumental activity is being pictured. But the I. A. I. pictures are depersonalized and decontextualized as far as specific personnel and locations are concerned. (1965:11)

Projective materials that can create feedback experience range from the Rorschach ink-blot to the intimate photographic essay of a man's life. The projective response can be one of free association from deeply submerged feelings or can be highly structured and self-consciously factual. In the course of a study all these levels of response might be drawn upon according to the needs of the research. We

---

[5] Private communication.

should select the most suitable projective tool. To do this projective responses should be viewed in their proper order of abstraction, from imagery of the subconscious to factual explanation of realistic data. It is important to keep in mind that there is a direct relationship between our tool and the nature of the informant's reponse. The more abstract the projective shape the less predetermined the area of the response becomes. This is why the ink-blot has proven so evocative of submerged feeling in psychological probings.

Here is an overview of the most frequently used projective tests:

Projective Testing Tool	*Levels of Expected Response*
	EXTREME ABSTRACTION
	Submerged feelings about self.
	Sexual emotions and fixations.
Rorschach Tests	Extremely free associations that dredge up thoughts passing through consciousness and subconsciousness.
	SEMIABSTRACTION
	Submerged feelings about self in relation to experiences in real world.
Thematic Apperception Tests	Free association about the significances of circumstances which could take place in the real world.
	GENERALIZED REPRESENTATION
	Concrete sentiments about circumstantial reality.
Defined Line Drawings	Free association about universal problems.
	Positive views about self with regard to the supernatural, universal or cultural values.
	LOWEST LEVEL OF ABSTRACTION
	Precise descriptive reportage.
	Sweeping encyclopedic explanations.
	Precise identification of event or circumstance.
	Noticeable lack of submerged psychological responses.
Clear Photographs of Familiar Circumstances	Noticeable lack of free association.
	BUT
	Factual representation of *critical* areas of the informant's life *can* trigger emotional revelations otherwise withheld, can release psychological explosions and powerful statements of values.

The TAT is the test most closely related to the possible use of photographs as projective stimuli in interviewing. This proximity suggests the use of photography to manufacture TAT material tailored for special uses. But if our purpose is to stimulate fantasy, substituting clear photographs for blurred TAT images will not work. Experimentally, I collaborated with a group at Cornell translating TAT pic-

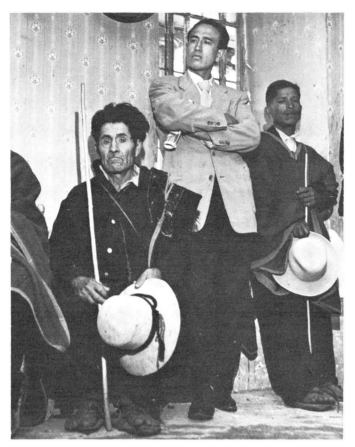

What makes an Indian in the Andes? Genetics? A frame of mind? A cultural way? Some of this subtlety can be verbalized, but much of the difference can also be seen. Political meeting in a small town in the Callejon de Hualas, Peru.

tures into photographs for a psychological study of projective responses. The results turned out to be entirely different from the TAT cards for, even at a glance, the testee would grasp and respond to the specific circumstances. The emphasis shifted away from imaginative story-telling to precise analysis of the photograph's documentary evidence.

Methodologically, the TAT concept could be modified to allow for significant projective responses using photographs. The shift would have to exploit the literal clear understanding of what was pictured in each circumstance. Instead of a multiple interpretation test you would have a projective questionnaire that could gauge an informant's attitudes and adjustments to structured experiences within his culture. It would be a valid testing tool in that you could confront any number of natives in the same way with exactly the same probes of their attitudes about their culture. "How do you feel? What pleases you in your life? What upsets you?"

The projective test made with photographs would have to operate on a very tangible level, where the informant would respond to a real circumstance, clearly recognizable. A possible example of this kind of projective testing might be a set of photographic cards showing classroom situations. These tests could be used to screen teachers for work among under-privileged children. Photographs could show rowdy students interrupting a class, a teacher shaking a Negro child in anger, or in the reverse, a teacher physically comforting a weeping Negro child. Scenes of this kind could be used to pretest a potential teacher's pattern of reaction, "How would you respond to these classroom situations?" Here the tangibility of the projective material would work in your favor.

In common with other culture-bound tests, one of the handicaps of the standard TAT is that it can fail to operate cross-culturally, simply because the visual triggers fall outside cultural familiarity. Could photography correct this fault? Only in part. Native made drawings, as the Spindlers' work points out, may do this job better. On the other hand, photography can greatly assist in producing culturally correct drawings for projective testing.

Robert Edgerton used drawings with the Menominee of Wisconsin to elicit responses about values in relation to acculturation levels, using the Spindler sample of sociocultural categories (Goldschmidt and Edgerton, 1961). But his experience with some of the drawings illustrates how important it is to have the cultural details correct. One of the test cards showed Menominees around a large drum, apparently dancing for tourists. The questions asked were about the values involved in these performances. Instead of giving relevant responses informants asked, "What is that drum?" The artist had mistakenly drawn a picture of Indians in dancing costumes worn only at public "pow-wows" dancing around a scared ceremonial drum. This so puzzled the informants that they could not answer the probing question.

The multiple choice opportunities offered by the ambiguous TAT images, could be accomplished with photographs in a cross-cultural projective test *if* the judgments exploited the tangible record, in the same way as did the screening material for teachers. Material probed for would have to be specific, rather than general. If the projective test were considered in this fashion, photography would certainly be the best way to assemble these examinations.

Changing sentiments of status in another culture might be explored by this type of photographic projective test. Again highly tangible situations would be photographed and assembled in various kits. For example, to explore "Who has status in a changing culture?" test cards could show the roles and interaction of the contemporary cast of village characters, both native and alien, native priests of various sects, native leaders, men of various castes and professions, foreign traders and intruders, Peace Corps workers, Navy personnel, tourists, personnel from the various diplomatic missions, and so forth. "Which of these men are most important? Which of these men are least important? Which groups do you associate with? Which groups do you most fear?" Even free association about this cast of characters would trigger sentiments on the existing social structure. In this fashion many sentiments could be examined systematically.

In the circumstance of rapid acculturation, classical modes can shift, upsetting the speculations of anthropology. We constantly need a fresh look, for culture is always emerging. Some classical values remain stationary, but others change completely. Photographs provide a way of making a fresh assessment.

An example of this occurred at one phase of Bernard J. Siegel's research at

Picuris, a small Indian Pueblo in New Mexico. I photographed for Dr. Siegel many aspects of community life—community work, agriculture, housing, and general ecology—gathering images for projective interviewing. An August fiesta presented us with an opportunity to record religious values. In particular, a beautiful deer dance appeared to yield rich photographic material. I was allowed to make a full record and then went on to document a traditional footrace that appeared much less impressive than the dance. Among the Pueblos, the deer dance has generally been looked upon as an important element in the dramatic ceremonial cycle. When Dr. Siegel photo-interviewed with the whole fiesta record, the deer dance pictures elicited only casual comments such as, "His moccasin is untied," or "The feathers are falling off his costume." But when a photograph was shown of the fiesta crowd moving to the footrace track the tone of the interview changed considerably from rather casual to solemn comments. And when informants were shown photographs of the running they went into elaborate metaphysical and social explanations, based on the religious significance and character of each runner. This interviewing made it clear that the dominant religious values were invested in the running rather than in this particular dance; verbal interviewing had not suggested this.

Dr. Siegel reports a set of responses which were elicited in relation to the same ceremonial occasion:

> Reactions to photographs were markedly different between males and females. Female respondents lingered over details of events associated with the Mass which preceded the Indian rituals. They were greatly concerned with the behavior of specific individuals, the holiness of the event, the role of the women in the Catholic-centered church activities, the qualities of the priest, and so forth. By contrast, they had little to say about details of the native processional, race, or dances. They revealed little knowledge about either belief or appropriate behavior in the latter contexts. Conversely, male informants had minimal knowledge or interest in Catholic-centered activities, but they commented at length on the right or wrong details of costume and behavior of individuals associated with native ceremonial. These data suggested the hypothesis that continued vitality of Catholic and Pueblo religious domains are the result, at least in large measure, of sex-linked differences in orientation to each of these systems before and after contact. They require a re-examination of Dozier's hypothesis of compartmentalization of belief to account for this phenomenon.[6]

The value of projective responses to photography is the powerful persuasion of *realism*. Often we think of psychological explosions in terms of symbolism; realism can be even more provocative. Not just photographic realism, but any real evidence can have the most explosive effect upon the witness—the dagger used in the murder, the intimate possessions of the victim.

In the First World War, I was once told, a German intelligence officer used the psychological pitfalls of realism to interrogate French officers on the Western Front. The trap for gaining intelligence was set by skilled hunters! A captured French officer would be treated with camaraderie: "We're all officers in the war together, comrades at arms in a deadly game. You're captured, so now relax. Let us drink together." The French officer was *not* questioned; instead he was invited down into a dugout to join a sumptuous meal, with wine, cigars, and good cheer.

[6] Personal communication.

But—on the wall was a map of the Western Front, with the armies of both sides located with colored pins. Throughout the meal the French officer eyed this deadly evidence, and in some instances, before the evening was through he would step to the map and compulsively correct the location of the pins revealing his own army's precise position—and then with horror step back. There is a fascination about evidence we intimately know and a common compulsion to express our knowledge.

Photographs are charged with unexpected emotional material that triggers intense feeling and divulges truth. It is probably more difficult to lie about a photograph than to lie in answer to a verbal question, for photographic scenes can cause violent feelings that are revealed by behavior, flushed faces, tense silence or verbal outbursts. The thematic qualities which can be found in photographic content, in intimate studies of the informant's life, evoke emotional statements of value—a positive "yes" and a positive "no." Using photographs projectively to reach these submerged areas requires tact and sensitivity to the emotions of the informant. Many times photographs contain triggers which the interviewer never realized. The most innocent picture can create an explosion that changes the whole character of the interview.

I once made a routine study of a pleasant village, which had once been a historical port. The file depicted old homes, docks, stores, scenes in the church and public school. We interviewed a local minister with this study. He was steeped in tradition, and gave us the classical view of the town—fine old families, old customs and values.

The interview ran its perfunctory course till we showed him pictures of a pie supper. He became flushed, laid down the pictures without comment and went on in his historical recitation. Then he picked up the pie supper pictures again and pointed to a smiling man holding up a pie for auction, "I shouldn't say this as a preacher, but I'd rather that man kill his wife than let her treat him the way she does! His wife is running with every loose man in the community . . . See that girl? She's pregnant. I know who the father is . . ." After this emotional break, the interview changed completely, and in heated words the minister gave us a very disturbing image of this traditional community.

So in one sense, photographs *do* function like Thematic Apperception cards, only that the stories told are about *real circumstances* involving real people.

7

Processing Nonverbal Evidence

URNING THE CONTENT of photographs into statistical and verbal data means converting the evidence of graphic description into statements that can become part of the verbal body of data and conclusion. Whether we analyze photographs by direct study or by the interpretation of photo-interviewing, we have not succeeded in completing research with the camera unless we can place the photographs aside in our final statement. That part of our study which has not been interpreted in this way remains *illustration,* not research conclusion.

This may be a shock to the sensitive photographer who places great significance on every nuance of his work. Certainly it was a shock to me when on my first anthropological research assignment I was told just this by the director of the project! "You know, John, when you finally present the results of your investigation, probably the publication will have no pictures."

This is not a rejection of the concept of a nonverbal text, and certainly illustrations *are* part of text. The scientific problem is that illustrations tend to be projective, indeed this is their provocative power. Natives invite you into the culture *on your terms,* a most rewarding accomplishment, educationally, since we are developing cultural empathy. But we must accept that this is education, not laboratory study.

A sketch of a hypothetical field study can clarify this evolution from documentary recording to integrated verbal data. Our projected assignment is the study of a mestizo-Indian market in Andean South America. An exhaustive photographic coverage has been completed based on time samples and a disciplined collecting and studying of material culture and sociometric patterns. On the basis of laboratory analysis an inventory of goods sold and bartered might be grouped as follows:

(1) Products from the highlands adjacent to the town (wool, wool textiles, grass rope, cabuya fiber rope, wheat, barley, quinoa, potatoes).

(2) Products from semi-tropical valley below the market town (fruit, bananas, platano, yuca roots, straw hats, clay dishes, ollas, calabash bowls, wooden spoons, hand forged tools).

(3) Products imported from outside the region (patent medicines, dyes, enamel dishes, metal cutlery, printed cotton yard goods, tinware, shoes, cheap

The Indians of Vicos trading with mestizo venders in the market in Marcara, Peru. Commercial relations between Indians and mestizos have been traditional, but under rapid change these relationships may be evolving. Photographs spanning a number of years could show if and how the Indian role is changing.

jewelry, plastic combs, barrettes, curlers, needles, spools of thread, colored embroidery floss, European tools and hardware, Swedish primus stoves, Coleman lanterns).

Visual analysis will indicate which of the products are handled by which of the merchants and traders. Photo-interviewing may yield a basis for estimating the relative value of goods traded in various categories. If our time sample covers the cycle of a year, seasonal variations will be apparent.

Key informants can certainly identify the major figures in the market place: How many vendors are Indian? How many are local mestizos? How many are traveling Indian or mestizo traders? How many are Europeans, Lebanese or Armenians, Germans? What is their position in the local economy?

These counts can be made quite accurately. Further we can observe directly from the photographs the differences in methods. Vendors from the sierra spread market cloths on the ground in a row, a certain distance from the more organized, or even permanent, stalls of the mestizo and European traders.

Photographic sweeps of the market made every half-hour from 5 A.M. to 9 A.M. can be counted upon to show the rise and fall of activity. Perhaps the peak is reached by 6:30 and by 7:30 trading will nearly be over; by 8:00, stalls are being packed up, carrying cloths loaded with wares; and by 9:00 the market is deserted except for scavenging dogs, two policemen, and a band of eight Indians sweeping the plaza under the direction or surveillance of the police. Or there may be two separate curves of activity, one for the high altitude Indian craftsmen traders, another later one for the vendors of lower altitude produce whose main customers are the local mestizo housewives and the servant boys who carry their market baskets.

In any case we can identify people from the pictures, with the help of an informant to give us the cues of costume—hats, ponchos, styles of blouses, skirts, belts. We can make a good approximation of the relative number of Indians from nearby, Indians from other areas, mestizos from the immediate area, mestizos from outside the area, any representatives of the town's local elite class. We can also check for distribution of sex roles in the different groups. Mestizo women may be clearly in charge of an entire branch of commerce, men of another. Perhaps there is a distinct group of quite well-dressed mestizo men. Who are these idlers? Who can afford the time to stand around in small groups? What social or political function does this aspect of the market represent? Children may have definite roles, or may be wandering about without responsibility, again the role being different for the different groups.

This is a review of the sorts of data found in a market place that can be studied by counting photographic elements, measuring the sociometric use of space, and comparing the time slices. Thus a full and systematic photographic coverage of the market gives us a model of the economy, the social structure, the role expectancies of the area.

Are figures determined by this sort of photographic analysis accurate? Is it possible to count every Indian in the market place by photography? Of course, the methods described are more useful for indicating proportion than absolute number. (Absolute number is elusive; an unverified story has it that Second World War sugar and coffee rationing turned up some 15,000 more Navajos than had been counted by the U.S. census takers two years earlier!) Photography is a sampling process and is subject to the same disciplines as other sampling processes; the more rigorous the sampling the closer we can approach statistical accuracy. Counts based on photographs are made scientifically useful by considering a plus-or-minus factor. The field-method question is: When we count heads photographically, can we make this margin of error less than when we use direct observation? Can we, with proper techniques of photographic counting, reduce this margin to a minimum? When we write down field notes we are computing on the spot, with no future chance of correcting our impressions. The photographic observation is computed in the laboratory, and any impressionism is always open to further checking as we develop more refined techniques of interpretation.

Research Design

The moment we think in terms of qualitative and quantitative comparisons, we face the problem of structured versus unstructured observation. Impulsive photography—often the most creative, often capturing the mood of a culture (an extremely difficult challenge)—cannot be depended upon to give us cultural elements that we can responsibly compare. Only like functional circumstances can be considered comparable, for example, spatial arrangements of eating the morning meal in one society as compared to another. Hence, if we are to make cultural measurements by comparison, we need to structure the way we observe and how we sample, or we will fail in our undertaking. We must devise a scheme of selectivity or there will be no opportunity for scientific comparison.

The problem of sampling is pertinent whether we are photographing or whether we are interviewing, and there is a considerable effort in field research to select a sample of informants in a comprehensive way, in order to gain a balanced view of a region. The issue of sampling leads us to the purpose of research design —to accomplish both balance and control of validity.

Systematic dissection and spot sampling are particularly crucial in studying the large regions and the super-communities encountered in urban anthropology. We must turn either to random sampling of material or samplings of significant clusters of material which advance study indicates may contain the data we are seeking. When we are working with small groups, our sampling might simply be every other home, as compared to a large area where we would sample every fifth, tenth, of fifteenth home or farmstead. Here the mathematical extent of our material would offer us a responsible impression. The design of the sample would depend largely on the circumstances. In Vicos, Peru, where I made a household inventory as a baseline of culture, the field director decided that every eighth house in this community of some two thousand inhabitants would give us a responsible profile. In this case the sample was random, based on the housing census numbers that existed in the project's file.

We can compute only quantitative facts. No matter how rich our photographic material is, our statistical recovery is limited to content that is countable, measurable, or scalable. A whole photographic view of a family sitting around the supper table is a tangible circumstance that can be accurately examined. On the other hand, an uncomputable photograph would be a family scene where visual identity and position is unclear, where shadow and light make dramatic patterns suggesting an emotional situation that may be projectively sensed rather than actually seen. Compared to this, consider what could be done with programmed views of a family table at breakfast, noon, and supper. Comparison of these mealtimes would offer many tangibles which could spell out reliable statements about the culture.

A structural approach to visible facts may seem to severely limit the opportunity for photographic recording, but as selective as these tangibles may seem, we can rarely use all of them in any one study. The wealth of measurable facts within cultural photographs is so enormous, that to work with them intelligently requires selecting only the most significant variables, gathering a large enough body of evidence to form patterns later in the research.

If we attempted to handle all the tangible content of an extensive photographic study, the computing process might become so unwieldy as to become in itself a defeat. The challenge of "total" documentation can only be approached with very small samples of field work. Generally, anthropological recordings are very selective and the product of extreme sampling.

Paul Ekman, director of the Nonverbal Research Center at Langley Porter Clinic in San Francisco, uses film for recording the total behavior of informants during an interview. On the average, Ekman has stated, it takes 24 hours of study to compute all the variables he is concerned with in a minute of film.[1] When we consider this minute shows just one individual sitting against a grid we can appreciate the deluge of material that could form the content of a saturated study of a family. Of course, Ekman is screening for specialized evidence. The degree to which we use photo content is controlled by what criteria of evidence we choose as essential in bearing out our conclusions.

We can read out of photographs, through measuring, counting, and comparing *all material items*—artifacts, tools, furniture, appliances, verbal documents, and works of art. We can compute *all circumstances* where we have control of literal identification through photo-interviewing, or control through repetitive samples that allow a reasonable integrity of cultural consistency, or circumstances selected by sampling designed to give a scientifically random view, to make a mathematically significant pattern.

This material can be seen and transcribed from photographic studies, and correlated in graphs and statistics with other evidence of family culture or whatever is the area of our concern. This level of data can be gathered in any number of homes recorded, in a way that creates large profiles of community and urban culture. Within the empirical experience, the same data can be extracted and interpreted validly and can become part of ethnographic record. The precision of the nonverbal message in any one culture allows for an intelligent reading out of this level of photographic content, thereby deepening the language of cultural description.

---

[1] Private communication.

The Practical Experience

Processing photographic content is a fundamental transition that makes it possible to think in terms of data, rather than illustrative image. You can look through photographs ceaselessly and arrive at no factual base unless some orderly process of abstraction takes place.

The first abstracting step is to take inventory. What evidence do you have? What did the camera witness? These questions should be open-ended. Before you review your records, all you have is a memory, a pervasive view of what has taken place. You can turn to your photographs as a check on memory, and you should consider your camera a control device to give you a further stabilization of real experience. Rarely do you know what is in your camera records, therefore you begin in a methodical manner.

One of the most significant processes in photographic computing is the selection of variables to track through your photographic records. Often the inability to recognize such signports leaves the task of computing so complex that it becomes self-defeating. Ideally these variables, so significant in the analysis of content, are decided upon in the saturated inventory where certain phenomena appear in quantities large enough to make statistical patterns possible, or where the interrelationship of certain variables appear to have responsible and significant meaning.

The second step goes beyond inventory and begins to build categorical structures from the classified material. You make judgments based on number of operations. The most tangible judgment is based on various quantities of visual elements, of ecological elements, of social groupings, of cultural possessions. Statistical count often provides the first categorical recovery from the photographic file.

In archeology certain characteristics of ceramics define the classification and age of a pot. In the cultural study stylistic clues are also a valid basis for differentiation. The presence of certain elements clearly identifies cultural influence. Likewise in a study of psychological phenomena in cultural circumstance, a relatively few behavioral variables might serve as a responsible index of the presence or absence of stress. This would also be true in studies of acculturation. Limited variables might prove to be diagnostically reliable measures of cultural change. "Count the people with sandals and you have counted the Indians" could prove true in a given market place.

Another level of judgment is based on the comparison of qualitative observations. Cultural circumstance can begin to take on concrete structure when differences are measured and characterizations made precise. For example, you will need to define the elements that constitute rustic dress, urban dress, cultural clutter and cultural simplicity, and so on, and the various transition points between the extremes. Content analysis of photographs reveals the actual patterns of a culture by condensing scattered evidence into schemes of statistical designs. These designs can become the basis for responsible judgments and verbal concepts about environment and human behavior.

Still another level of judgment is derived from the correlation of variables of activity. Where and how often does a selected type of behavior appear? An analysis of these variables is a study of selected elements of photographic content which you feel give depth understanding to your field of research.

The simplified categories under which a photographic file may be arranged for general use or for storage, may prove inadequate for the refined measure of detailed clues for rapid tracking and comparing of behavioral variables, such as spatial measure and body posture. To isolate all factors requires an exhaustive cross-filing pattern. This multiplication of photographic file materials could become impossibly cumbersome and financially prohibitive. The McBee punch card system provides an ideal solution. Once the content analysis has turned up the research variables, further study can be made directly with the chronological contact print file by mounting the contact prints or sheet of contact prints directly on punch cards. Any number of variables can be rapidly pulled from the master file by needling through the punch cards to drop out *all* contact sheets that contain the variable. This allows for study of specialized elements in the file without disturbing the context of the chronological environmental experience. This guards against a common failing in fragmented research—losing sight of the whole. We turn to photography in the first place in an effort to get a holistic overlook. It would be self-defeating to lose this view by the process of abstraction.

A third step in moving from visual image to scientific conclusion is to condense the evidence found through volume analysis or tracking of variables into statistical tables, charts, and diagrams. This is another purpose of our computing process that allows us to view the photographic data in strictly numerical and diagrammatic terms. When we reach this point, we can move our photographic contents smoothly into the scientific record of anthropology.

Intangible Content: A Second Level of Data Found within Anthropological Photographs

Reliable use of data found in photographs requires the division of content into two distinct categories and a method to process each of these areas. If this is not done, either of two equally disturbing developments can take place. On the one hand, what is drawn from the photographs may become drastically limited in order to conform to a concept of scientific comparability. Or we can attempt to use our reaction to the photographic content as a whole as a source of data, but without some basis of control, this could produce highly impressionistic evidence that would find little place in a scientific conclusion.

To avoid either eventuality we must define levels of content. One level, which I will refer to as the tangible, deals directly with *material culture* and *sociometric dimensions,* and in a series of responsibly related photographs the *order of occurences* and *change in spatial relationships.* This level we have discussed in detail in the first half of this chapter. The second level is involved with the *effects* of both material and sociometric possibilities, as well as with the effects of multitudes of unseen pressures of culture and environment in general. In the case of our research, the effects of rapid social change might be a particularly significant order of content found within this second level.

In this conglomerate level we consider the artifacts of culture as they are affected by the tempo of each family's life, or we attempt to relate the material scheme of the homes to the function of each family. The working problem of scientific interpretation lies in computing the factual description of artifacts and sociometric arrangement, *then* fitting this digested data into an equally responsible judgment of the over-all significance of these parts to the whole meaning of each family's existence.

Methodologically we have two performances. The first is a fairly mechanical direct accounting of material elements and cultural arrangements. The second is a correlation of our sense of over-all pattern of the family culture with *all* levels of available research data. This correlation can rarely be made by any controlled counting or measuring but rather by making judgments which can qualify the visual character of each photographed family.

For comprehensive research conclusions, the research design should accommodate these two levels of significance. The first level of data presents no major problem. It can be computed by an impartial counting, measuring, and identification of visible schemes of material culture and can be translated practically into statistical significance. The second level, which may contain the richest evidence of culture and personality, presents itself in a more or less nebulous manner that is a challenge to scientific evaluation.

Many anthropologists have attempted to use the bouquet of culture which is felt to be present in photographs. The common experience has been that this photographic conglomeration defies validation by any of the controlled systems by which other humanistic data can be evaluated. When this uncontrollability is discovered the tendency is not to use photographic data. Possibly this rejection would not take place if the open-ended quality of photographic opportunity were exploited for this very character.

The synthesizing process, the function of intuition in human understanding, is certainly not rejected by science; indeed, science is largely dependent upon it. The function of controls and measurements, where they can be devised, is to provide checks and tests to temper and rationalize the flight of thought. Do we not value the "sense" that the anthropologist accumulates about the character of each culture with which he works? This is a subjective and intuitive sense, and is uncontrolled and unvalidated only to the extent that it necessarily goes beyond the consideration of factors that can be controlled and verified.

What is the value of the fieldworker's reaction to and interaction with the group he is studying, quite aside from his accomplishment of administering tests and obtaining specified information or taking a series of pictures? Is not the interaction the basis of personal insight, and a possible source of interpretation of questionnaires, tests, and photographs? Any means of judgment about cultural phenomena made within the framework of a study would seem to be of great importance.

If this could be true and applicable, then also the character of each file of photographic family studies could be of equal importance. But like the fieldworker's impressions, composite photographic records operate on a different level and have a different function from that of the mass of controllable data on which research conclusions more formally rest.

There is really no great problem in using the whole photographs or sets of photographs in our research, if we can incorporate them into the methodology so that their genuine character can and will be responsibly used.

How can we use the rich intangibles of photographs such as the dramatic picture of a rock-bound fishing village in a storm? Count the houses? Draw a schematic map of the town? Make a typology of the kinds of fishing boats clustered under the lee of the breakwater? Obviously this does not exploit the wealth of content contained in a record of this kind. The key to its richness is in the emotional quality of the imagery. Emotional for whom? The fieldworker?

The riddle the picture poses is: what are the attitudes of the villagers to this wild scene? A fisherman's response might be very different from our own "Great lobster weather! A typical fall storm. When the wind and seas drop, we'll put out our pots." Or, "If it weren't for a good blow now and then, the government never would keep our breakwater in repair." On the other hand, under probing, still another fisherman might confess a fear of the sea that has hounded him all his life. Or a fisherman's wife might blurt out her life-long terror for "our men-folk on the banks." At another extreme an old-timer might express a sophisticated love for the wind and wild water. The provocative photograph *can* be a key to the ethos of a people. Through photo-interviewing we can discover the fears, mystic beliefs, and aesthetic values of the native culture.

A second approach carries this definition process a step further. In much the same manner as the native informant, the social scientist can also be interviewed with intangible as well as tangible data. In 1953, Margaret Mead described to me how she approached the scientific use of photographs at one level of a child development study. The research team sat around a conference table which was covered with a large number of photographs of a specialized area of the research. The photographs provided a saturated stream of images. The team would express their impressions, informed and stimulated by the multiple evidence, and often new concepts and correlations would be born.[2]

In considering such a reading, I can see that the saturated character of the photographic evidence acts as its own control force, which offers a stabilizing view of action and behavior, not unlike film, except in this case the time coverage could be considerably more comprehensive than in one detailed film. I can appreciate that Margaret Mead was seeking an accurate characterization of behavior that could only be obtained through a very extensive personality inventory and an equally expansive time sample. The psychological effect of looking intensely at multitudes of related photographs is that they do superimpose themselves into a few characteristic images. Hence typical models of behavior and environment can be recognized.

Paul Byers (see Chaps. 4 and 5) carried this technique into an action methodology in which the photographer makes intensive records precisely for research and brings back an organized photo-data file that can be used for saturated analysis in the laboratory. This method depends upon "large numbers of pictures of interactional events to record minimal changes or differences which may be crucial to an analysis of events on a micro-cultural level but which would not be precisely

---

[2] Private communication.

observed without the use of the camera." (Mead, 1963:178) Byers' comprehensive and intensive photographic view, presented in an organized way to viewers who are themselves specialists, could have the same effect as the over-view accomplished by Dr. Mead, but on a more structured level. Again, authenticity would come from the completeness of the photographic sample, but Byers' anthropological grouping of the records could be employed to carry the analytic process further.

The point of this technique is that records of micro-cultural or macro-cultural episodes invariably contain suggestive intangible and fleeting impressions that cannot be handled simply by orderly frame-by-frame analysis. Using photographs in this saturated way can give the anthropologist authentic and new empirical impressions that trigger insights that could otherwise be obtained only by the anthropologist himself returning to the field.

8

Computing and Interpreting the Cultural Inventory

JOHN ROBERTS, OF Cornell University, made the pioneering effort in controlled cultural inventory in his complete recording of three Navajo households near Ramah, New Mexico (1951). He used photography in his publication to illustrate the surface character of the hogans, but the elaborate listing of objects, to our knowledge, was done entirely with a notebook. This study remains impressive and continues to excite speculation as to what could be concluded from such effort, for Dr. Roberts has left up to the reader what the implications of family property might be.

The value of the inventory is based upon the assumption that the "look" of a home shows a significant relationship to the way the family is coping with the problems of life. John Honigmann states this propostion:

> An inspection of material culture may contribute insights into character structure and reveal emotional qualities. Product analysis entails examining utilitarian constructions, like houses and toboggans, to determine the values they embody, as revealed, for example, in careless or perfectionistic construction. The proportion of non-utilitarian objects to utilitarian objects in a culture may also be meaningful. Type and number of possessions may reveal drives and aspirations in a class structured community (1954:134).

Jurgen Ruesch and Weldon Kees emphasize the importance of the use of objects in the psychological make-up of people and cultures.

> The selection of objects and the nature of their grouping constitute nonverbal expressions of thought, need, conditions, or emotions. Thus, when people shape their surroundings, they introduce man-made order. (1956:94)

> Foremost in the array of things that men have ordered are the objects with which they surround themselves in their own homes. . . . [Though] not everyone is fortunate enough to live in a structure built to meet the demands of his own taste . . . every building indicates in some way whether or not it is representative of those who live in it. This is particularly true about interiors, where the nature and arrangement of possessions say a great deal about their owners' views of existence (1956:132).

Home of a tobacco farmer in Tolima, Colombia. Is this a pre-Columbian kitchen, or are there many European innovations? Analysis of the cultural inventory can clarify such questions that rest in the literal image of material culture.

And Edward T. Hall comments on the use of space:

> . . . the inside of the Western house is organized spatially. Not only are there special rooms for special functions—food preparation, eating, entertaining and socializing, rest, recuperation and procreation—but for sanitation as well. *If,* as sometimes happens, either the artifacts or the activities associated with one space are transferred to another space, this fact is immediately apparent. People who "live in a mess" or a "constant state of confusion" are those who fail to classify activities and artifacts according to a uniform, consistent, or predictable spatial plan (1966:97).

The cultural inventory offers one of the richest pools of data which can be gathered photographically. Just what *can* be studied responsibly in the details of an American home? Here are some of the questions that can be asked in relation to the cultural inventory:

WHAT IS THE ECONOMIC LEVEL?

> Homes reflect economic adequacy or poverty. The condition of the furniture, rugs, wallpaper, curtains, rate a house economically.

Economic stress often shows throughout most of the home's possessions, and economic stress necessarily limits the range of *choice* in the determining of style.

WHAT IS THE STYLE?

Home styles have a great deal to do with life styles; some ways of life are associated with one style, other ways with another. Some styles are mixed and overlap, others are mutually exclusive.

Some styles reflect regional background, with their prototypes in the mid-Western farm house or the California ranch home. Many American home styles can be traced back to European models, the "manor", the London townhouse, the intimately elegant "villa".

Some styles have names which represent quite specific models in materials, aesthetics, and use: for example, Early American, Traditional, Modern, Louis Quinze, Empire, Provincial, Danish Modern, Japanese, Hollywood Moorish.

Each area has a going value system, as in San Francisco, a Nob Hill apartment, a Haight Street pad, and a Pacifica tract home call up entirely different images.

Style (or the lack of it) often places the household in the class and status structure.

WHAT ARE THE AESTHETICS OF DECORATION?

Not only pictures on the wall, but every object of decoration, each item selected and kept for its own sake, is a clue to the owners' value system. These reflect:

Religious expression,

Ethnic identity or affinity,

Political affiliation or sentiment.

They also reflect aesthetic judgments:

"High-brow"—educated, sophisticated;

"Middle-brow"—striving for cultural status;

"Low-brow"—taste of the "common man".

They may have a subject-content focus:

Nature-oriented, to the open spaces, mountains, seas, forests, gardens, wild animals;

Socially oriented, scenes of history, humanity, children, dogs, cats;

Or not subject-oriented, nonrepresentational, interested in form or color rather than content.

They may show a distinct preference for one or several styles:

Traditional styles: biblical, Greek, Roman, Renaissance art, old masters, established "masterpieces";

Progressively oriented: modern art, abstraction, non-objectivity, industrial ornaments, parts of machines as elements of industrial design, beauty as function;

Ethnically oriented: native art, Oriental or exotic designs and ornaments, primitive art.

WHAT ARE THE ACTIVITIES OF THE HOUSEHOLD?

The house may be only to eat and sleep in, or it may be the scene of and the product of, a great deal of activity, work, play, and socialization.

Or it may give evidence of self-expression of its inhabitants:

Craft, "do-it-yourself" home furnishings, needlework, textiles, model-making;

Artwork, drawings, paintings, sculpture—(classical or modern? representational or non-objective?) made by the inhabitants or their personal circle of friends; school art of the children;

Is the home design a standardized copy of magazine taste, or does it show inventiveness of these people?

Are there organic interests—plants, birds, goldfish, pets, nature collections?

Is there music in the house?

Music produced here, piano or other instruments, sheet music, music stands;

Music listened to, record player, stacks or cabinets of records, Hi-Fi equipment, radio, television.

Are sports and games represented?

Evidence of active sports, equipment, trophies, games, toys, for children, for adults, or both;

Evidence of sports interest (spectator sports), pictures of Willie Mays, etc., sports schedules, newspaper sports page, sports magazines.

What is the level of literate interest in the household?

Quantity and choice of books, standard works, classics, text books, best sellers, detective stories, extensive library on one or several subjects, poetry, art books, avant-garde works—whatever;

Magazines—the whole range from *Look* and *Life* through women's magazines, sports magazines, news magazines, political comment, girlie magazines, all help to categorize the mental concerns of the inhabitants;

Newspapers, funny books, religious tracts, ditto.

Is the home the place for social life? For the family only, or for the entertainment of friends?

Is eating a major focus of family values? Food technology and attitudes are often culturally determined, often reflected in kitchen tools and the inventory of the closet shelves.

WHAT IS THE PSYCHOLOGICAL CHARACTER OF ORDER?

The order of the home reflects the means by which people pattern their lives. "A place for everything and everything in its place," represents an ideal of mastery over the material objects of life's circumstances. This could be evidence of one kind of organized personality, or it might represent a psychological compulsion.

Housekeeping is fundamentally the job of getting things back into their places, a job of classification, by use, by size, by shape, by aesthetic considerations. Piling and dumping are intermediate stages in the classification process.

Mess is the clutter and chaos that accumulates as things are *not* in a reasonable place—either because the reason of their ordering is not established (which represents confusion and disorder in the minds of the people and may represent a cultural ineptitude in the face of cultural chaos or rapid change) or because the housekeeping function is not being fulfilled, for whatever reason of insufficiency of time, energy, health or motivation.

Another form of clutter occurs, even when things are "in their place," if there are too many things or if the basis of their ordering is unreasonable or interferes in some way with function. Space is definitely needed for various functions, and though the definition of that need varies with different cultures, each culture prescribes the acceptable limits in its own terms, and acceptable housekeeping in each culture sees that this space is provided.

WHAT ARE THE SIGNS OF HOSPITALITY AND RELAXATION?

In our culture, by cues of placement and ordering of furniture, we know when we come into a room whether we are expected to remain standing or sit down, and if we are to sit down, where, and how. Furniture is placed to offer hospitality or refuse it. A bookcase may invite you to help yourself, or it may prompt you to ask first, or it may be so forbidding you would never think of doing more than looking.

The different styles of furnishings present different values of hospitality. Sometimes roles are clearly defined in formal fashion. Sometimes informality is given the higher value. The attitude expressed in "If I'd a knowed you was comin' I'd have baked a cake!" has its expression in many details of furniture choice and arrangement.

In evaluating the cultural cues, we have to ask, what does this kind of a chair mean in this particular setting?

Report of a Photographic Research Project

The rest of this chapter will be devoted to an account of the photographic study I recently made of 22 Indian households, part of a research project on American Indian Urban Integration directed by Dr. James Hirabayashi of San Francisco State College.

There are approximately 10,000 Indians relocated in the San Francisco Bay Area. How do they adapt to the urban environment? What are their methods of adjustment and acculturation? Why do some succeed in the urban center while many fail and return to their reservations? The very mass of statistical data to be studied presented the need for computerized techniques, questionnaires, and psychological tests in conjunction with conventional interviewing. Some 50 researchers were involved, all working under severe limitations of time and funds with which to complete the study so that it could be integrated into national research on migration and human displacement—a primary concern of the National Institute of Mental Health which sponsored the program.

This was an anthropological and a psychological problem having to do with changing cultures of Indians from many diverse tribes. Methodologically there was a real challenge to retain the ethnographic view in the strictly urban setting. Could models of the new urban Indian culture be drawn? How could cultural description be systematically correlated with the larger statistical findings?

Photography was chosen as a tool for synchronizing ethnographic description. This offered the project a number of tangible supports—a variety of recordings, accomplished by photographic observation in depth of a fairly small sample, and a return of data that could be processed by statistical analysis. This meant that a correlation between the questionnaire data and the ethnographic descriptions could be established. This presented the challenges reviewed in Chapter 8, recovering and applying the factual levels of photographic recording, and then going beyond to correlate the holistic schemes of the culture gathered in the open view of the relocated Indian's life.

The Indian homes were clearly defined units where comparable routine recordings could be made. The cultural inventories thus assembled offered an opportunity for observing and measuring acculturation and analysing schemes of success and failure in relocation. We were concerned with *what* is in the Indian home, with its quality and condition, the manner in which it is ordered, and its relationship to the Indian family.

Since the sample of 22 households was too small to offer the validity of random sampling procedures, the families to be photographed were selected on the basis of rapport and cooperation, but also the fieldworkers involved did their best to provide range and variety in tribal background, economic level, age, length of time in the area, and the methods of relocation—self-initiated, or government sponsored for employment or for training.

After contact and sufficient rapport had been established by one of the project's interviewers, each of the families (with one exception) was photographed on a single visit with consent and by appointment. The fieldworker was present as well as myself, the photographer. In all cases living rooms and kitchens were thoroughly photographed. In all but four households one or more bedrooms were also covered. The focus was chiefly upon the contents of the household and its arrangement, with wide-angle shots to show placement of the various items and furniture and the relationship between rooms, and with close-up shots to show areas of particular interest such as mantles and bureaus and the tops of television sets where small but presumably valued objects were collected.

In the course of the session I made informal portraits and group portraits of the family—for the benefit of the family as well as the project. Beyond this the normal activities taking place were photographed if the situation remained fluid and cooperative. In any case the photography was not allowed to push beyond the tolerance of the family involved and was discontinued if it was perceived as threatening. This occurred in two instances, though in both cases the major part of the coverage had been made before this point was reached.

The pictures were taken with a Leica by available light in the belief that this would give the most accurate rendering of actual living conditions. This is undoubtedly the case, yet it proved to have the disadvantage of limiting detail in poorly lit

Clothes rack in a home in Vicos, Peru. What changes first in the evolving culture? Clothing, technology, sanitation? The cultural inventory can be a definitive measure of progress and degree of change in the domestic life of the Vicosinos.

homes. For certain types of recording bounced strobe light might have greatly increased the depth of focus and made reading of detail easier (see Chap. 9).

From one to two 36-exposure rolls of 35 mm film were taken of each household. These were contact printed, and six to ten key pictures were enlarged from each set. For analysis both the enlargements and the contacts were studied, the latter with the help of magnifying glass.

Analysis of the Data Collected

The study consisted of an inventory of the objects in each of the houses, a comparison of the inventories with each other, and a comparison of the inventories with what was known about the families from the interview and questionnaire data. Finally there was an attempt to bring these together with the general concerns of the project. This was done by indicating how the houses reflected the attitudes toward "Indianness" and the attitudes toward the dominant culture, and by attempting to identify the value systems by which the various families operate in the urban setting. My wife made the detailed analysis of the inventory, prepared the charts of comparisons between the photographic data and the questionnaire and interview data, and worked closely with me on the report.

A first and over-all impression of the photographs was that these households are almost all well equipped—in variety if not in quality—with the essential items. Anyone with a memory of the thirties, or a knowledge of rural poverty, or a familiarity with houses on any of the remote Indian reservations, is apt to be impressed that every family has a refrigerator as well as a kitchen sink, gas or electric stove, and bathroom. Bathrooms were not photographed, but no family in the sample had to share theirs with another family, as is the case in many urban slums. All but two households show television sets—and one of these acquired one soon after. Nevertheless, the range of quality and adequacy of the furnishings is considerable.

In the absence of a general study of the contents of American households, we cannot say how these compare with the national image. In search of that image we turned to the women's magazines but found that their standards of elegance leave all but possibly two or three of these homes far behind. But the Montgomery Ward catalog does provide models—almost specific ones for several homes—and its range of styles and prices in many articles of furniture proved a valuable guide to relative values.

The inventory for each family consisted of a listing and description of furnishings and visible possessions, including quality, condition, material, and style, where relevant. The sample inventory following gives an idea of the sort of data which could be gathered by direct examination of the pictures.

Inventory: Laguna Family

MAJOR FURNISHINGS
upholstered sofa and matching chair
    (Back of sofa shows this was originally upholstered in large-figured Persian-scene tapestry material; now covered with mottled pattern; long bureau scarf with embroidered edge covers back of sofa, Pendleton blanket covers back of chair, worn cloths on arms of chair)
heavy wooden dining room table
old kitchen table
four light metal frame, plastic seat, chairs
wooden chair by TV
three double beds, all with chenille spreads
crib, moderately priced
inexpensive chest of drawers, ragged bureau scarf, and large round mirror
Venetian blinds and drapes to floor in living room
small worn rugs

USE OF SPACE
large room divided between living room space (sofa out across the room, facing television) and dining room-workshop space with table, chairs, and kitchen-type cabinets; dining-room table used by children for homework; books, etc., piled on cabinets
two double beds in one bedroom
one double bed and crib in second
kitchen work area off dining room, very compact

COMMAND OF URBAN TECHNOLOGY
large double-oven gas stove with timer
large refrigerator
cabinets and work counter built-in
small television on stand
Taylor-Tot stroller
wind-up alarm clock
lights in dining end but not in living room end of big room

ORDER—CLEANLINESS, NEATNESS, CONSISTENCY, AND STYLE:
kitchen spotless, everything put away
floors clean
miscellaneous objects piled, freshly ironed shirts hanging on cabinet in dining area
cartons for storage in bedroom corner, thermos on bureau
back of sofa exposed showing older upholstery
style—essentially utilitarian, unpretentious

LITERATE CULTURE
set of books, probably inexpensive encyclopedia
school books
newspapers

ART, MUSIC
large picture of aircraft carrier in frame
plaque of horse's head inside a horse-shoe
two wall plaques, (made in school?)
one photo-portrait with glass frame
school photo-portraits in cardboard frames, snapshots

SPORTS, TOYS
dolls and animals on ledge above living room window
doll in crib, other toys
child's rocking chair with music box attached
trophy for basketball

CHRISTIAN RELIGIOUS ITEMS
none

INDIAN OBJECTS
two woven ceremonial belts
rattle
three rather plain kachinas
striped Pendleton blanket, woman's plaid Pendleton blanket with fringe
abalone shell[1]

"SHRINE" AREA
dummy mantle (no fireplace) on one side of living room, basketball trophy in
    center, photo portraits on either side, pair of baby moccasins at far left, horse's
    head in horseshoe and small ceramic animal at far right
picture of aircraft carrier is centered above mantle, two snapshots tucked in corner
a foot or so away on either side of the mantle there are hanging, at the right a
    kachina and a rattle with a woven belt draped over them, at the left two ka-
    chinas and another woven belt.

---

[1] While not an exclusively Indian item, abalone shells from the west coast have been
trade goods for centuries and are valued by many Indian groups for use in jewelry and sacred
objects.

The first two categories of the inventory, major furnishings and command of urban technology, formed the basis for a comparison of the households in terms of quality and condition of furnishings. This proved fairly easy to do. The poorest homes were obviously the poorest, the best furnished were obviously the best. In between there was some confusion because households with distinctly different styles or taste are not strictly comparable, and the viewer's preference for one or the other style may enter into such a judgment.

As an aid in arriving at an over-all rating for the households, we took a close look at major comparable items. Sofas were the most prominent feature in all the living rooms of the sample. They ran the gamut from obviously battered, through the shabbily covered, through those with neatly tucked-in chenille or hob nail spread, to quite a few in good enough condition to be left uncovered, culminating in an elegant three-piece sectional in the home of a retired Sioux couple, the rounded corner section separated from the two side sections by matching polished hardwood step-tables. In one home a sofa is already made up as a bed, and in another home we have a boy all tucked in to go to sleep on the sofa. Whether the latter was a permanent arrangement or temporary, there is little question that sofas often double as beds. Chairs were of more varieties and seemed to be in somewhat better condition than sofas; possibly as less expensive than sofas, and less versatile, they are more easily acquired or disposed of.

Condition of the kitchens usually paralleled the condition of the house or apartment itself. Sink and cupboards usually represent equipment that comes with the house and therefore reflect the age of the house. Bedrooms, though not as thoroughly photographed as other parts of the house, proved to be points of fairly sharp demarcation—both in terms of style and of order.

Based on the actual pieces of furniture in the pictures we drew up five point scales of quality for several key categories:

SOFAS AND EASY CHAIRS
1. uncovered, wear and tear showing
2. covered with cheap or shabby spread
3. covered with good spread or blanket
4. uncovered, good condition
5. good condition, matched set

BEDS
1. lacks spread or lacks pillow case
2. shabby spread
3. good spread or quilt
4. good spread plus headboard
5. fancy spread and/or headboard and/or matching chest of drawers

KITCHEN SINKS AND CUPBOARDS
1. open sink, open shelves
2. units uncoordinated, skimpy, or ancient
3. units coordinated but not enclosed
4. units built-in, enclosed, ample
5. fancy units built-in, enclosed, ample

TABLE I

RANKING AND GROUPING OF HOUSEHOLDS ON THE BASIS OF
QUALITY AND CONDITION OF FURNISHINGS

Group I	Mostly makeshift, cheap or old; meager.	1. Pomo I 2. Pomo II
Group II	Mostly serviceable but graceless, utility more important than style; making do.	3. Eskimo II 4. Eskimo I 5. Hualapai-Navajo 6. Sioux I 7. Sioux II 8. Sioux III
Group III	Reasonably good, nothing basic lacking (except for very recent arrivals), frugal, modest, but selective.	9. Laguna 10. Navajo 11. Kiowa I 12. Kiowa II 13. Kiowa III 14. Kiowa-Eskimo
Group IV	Generally well furnished, ample; an eye to comfort and hospitability; not too particular about style, but some flair.	15. Miwok 16. Kiowa-Choctaw 17. Sioux IV 18. Sioux V 19. Basque-Rincon
Group V	Well furnished, highly selective, matched, with definite image in mind.	20. Italian-Seminole 21. Chippewa-Tutunai 22. Sioux VI

This is essentially the process used by Lloyd Warner in arriving at his grouping of social class (1949), or Russell Lynes in his characterizations of "highbrow, middlebrow, and lowbrow" in American taste (1957). We move from descriptive inventory to comparison, to establishment of a relevant typology. Of course neither Warner's nor Lynes' scale would do since our sample was so different from theirs, and since scales of this kind are very specific and soon outdated.

With these scales as guide lines, and referring back to the pictures themselves as well as the inventories so that the over-all look of the homes would be in mind, we were able to place the households in an approximate order from the poorest to the best in terms of quality and condition of furnishings by our understanding of the standards of the dominant culture (see Table I). Throughout the tables and the discussion that follows, the families are identified by tribal background, with the wife's tribe named first when husband and wife come from different groups; where there is more than one family from the same tribe, the most recent arrival is numbered "I," the next "II," and so forth.

This table and the correlative tables which follow are presented primarily to illustrate the movement of data from the photographic record to the abstraction of statistical design. The information in the tables is from the group of families we

TABLE II

VARIOUS ASPECTS OF STYLE COMPARED WITH QUALITY AND CONDITION OF FURNISHINGS

Vertical (row) axis label: **QUALITY AND CONDITION OF FURNISHINGS**

		QUANTITY		ORDER		FORMALITY			SELECTIVITY			STYLE		
		few things ←→	many	dis-order ←→	order	infor-mal ←→		for-mal	un-select ←→		se-lect	circum-stantial	conven-tional	per-sonal
I	Pomo I		x	x		x			x			x		
	Pomo II	x			x		x		x			x		
II	Eskimo II	x			x	x				x		x		
	Eskimo I	x			x			x				x		
	Hualapai-Navajo		x	x		x			x			x		
	Sioux I	x			x	x			x			x		
	Sioux II	x			x		x			x		x		
	Sioux III		x		x		x			x		x		
III	Laguna		x		x		x			x		x		
	Navajo		x		x			x		x		x		
	Kiowa I	x			x		x				x		x	
	Kiowa II	x			x		x				x		x	
	Kiowa III		x		x		x				x		x	
	Kiowa-Eskimo		x		x		x				x			x
IV	Miwok		x		x	x				x				x
	Kiowa-Choctaw		x		x	x				x				x
	Sioux IV		x		x		x			x			x	
	Sioux V	x			x		x			x			x	
	Basque-Rincon		x		x			x			x			x
V	Italian-Seminole	x			x			x			x		x	
	Chippewa-Tutunai		x		x			x			x		x	
	Sioux VI	x			x			x			x		x	

TABLE III

TRIBAL BACKGROUND OF WIFE COMPARED WITH QUALITY
AND CONDITION OF FURNISHINGS

		TRIBAL BACKGROUND*			
		West Coast	South- west	Southern Plains	Northern Plains	Caucasian
QUALITY AND CONDITION OF FURNISHINGS	I	Pomo I Pomo II				
	II	Eskimo II Eskimo I	Hualapai- Navajo		Sioux I Sioux II Sioux III	
	III		Navajo Laguna	Kiowa I Kiowa II Kiowa III Kiowa- Eskimo		
	IV	Miwok		Kiowa- Choctaw	Sioux IV Sioux V	Basque- Rincon**
	V				Chippewa- Tutunai Sioux VI	Italian- Seminole**

* Tribes are grouped by regions, west to east, roughly in inverse relation to length of contact with Anglo-American culture.
** Caucasian wives are both American born of recent European extraction.

photographed. The tables are only suggestive of the findings of the relocation study as a whole. As you study these tables, it is well to remember that you are looking at specific photographic elements that have been systematically examined and the data from them translated into chart form.

The ranking in Table I may be considered as a rough index of the relative material acculturation of these 22 families, or of the material levels on which their urban adjustment is being made. But there are other bases of comparison to be gained from examination of the photographs. Some of these are presented in Table II, chiefly as a descriptive modifier of the groupings in Table I. Here each household is rated on a three point scale for quantity of possessions, order, formality, and selectivity—and "style" is categorized as circumstantial, conventional or personal. It should be noted, of course, that in most of these categories, either the second or the third place on the three point scale may be considered most desirable, depending upon the value system; for example, a moderate degree of disorder may be considered preferable to complete order which could be considered compulsive or inhospitable. For this reason a clear pattern of correlation between these aspects of style and the quality and condition of furnishings is not to be expected. Yet a degree of correlation is indicated by the almost empty boxes in the upper right and lower left of each category. In general we may say the table suggests that the higher ranking families have greater choice and control of the style of their households.

The remainder of the tables present a comparison between the "look" of the relocated Indian homes derived from the photographs and four variables that affect the success of adjustment on relocation. That these variables—tribal background, time in the Bay Area, the education of the wife, and income level—are influences conditioning success is not surprising—indeed, they could be anticipated. What the tables show is how consistently the pattern of cultural inventory reflects these reasonable conditions of success. For the tables, each of these variables, drawn from questionnaire and interview data, is broken down into a five point scale. With the five part grouping from Table I on one side and one of these variables on the other we have a two dimensional grid, and correlation is indicated by the degree of clustering around the diagonal from upper left to lower right.

Table III shows how acculturation has moved from east to west. The tribes from which the families come are grouped by regions from west to east, roughly in inverse relation to the length of contact with Anglo-American culture. It is quite clear that Indians with longer tribal contact have made better urban adjustment. Among the most successful are the two families with Caucasian wives, though the husband of one is a California Indian; marriage to a Caucasian undoubtedly accelerates urban domestic acculturation. The position of the West Coast Miwok family reflects a rather unique economic success and extended urban experience. The low

TABLE IV

TIME IN THE BAY AREA COMPARED WITH QUALITY AND
CONDITION OF FURNISHINGS

		TIME IN THE BAY AREA			
		Less than 1 year	1 to 3 years	4 to 9 years	10 to 20 years	Over 20 years
QUALITY AND CONDITION OF FURNISHINGS	I		Pomo I Pomo II			
	II	Sioux I Sioux II	Eskimo II Eskimo I	Hualapai-Navajo Sioux III		
	III	Kiowa I Kiowa II	Kiowa III Kiowa-Eskimo	Navajo		
	IV			Kiowa-Choctaw Sioux IV Basque-Rincon	Miowok Sioux V	
	V				Italian-Seminole	Chippewa-Tutunai Sioux VI

Note: Laguna data uncertain.

TABLE V

EDUCATION OF WIVES COMPARED WITH QUALITY AND CONDITION OF FURNISHINGS

		EDUCATION OF WIVES			
		None	1st–4th grade	5th–10th grade	11th–high school grad.	Beyond or special
QUALITY AND CONDITION OF FURNISHINGS	I	Pomo I Pomo II				
	II		Eskimo I Eskimo II		Hualapai- Navajo Sioux III	Sioux I— nurses aide Sioux II— Haskell
	III			Navajo Kiowa II	Kiowa I Kiowa III	Kiowa- Eskimo- Haskell
	IV			Kiowa- Choctaw	Miwok Sioux IV Sioux V Basque- Rincon	
	V			Chippewa- Tutunai	Italian- Seminole	Sioux VI- Haskell

Notes: Laguna—no information. Haskell Institute, Lawrence, Kansas, is one of the oldest federal Indian boarding high schools and offers advanced vocational courses.

position of three of the Sioux families, as compared with the Kiowa families, reflects in this instance the economic insecurity of these Sioux in contrast to the young Kiowas who happen to have the advantage of small but dependable student stipends from the Bureau of Indian Affairs. It could also reflect a contrast in the historical course of acculturation of the tribes, for the Sioux contact, though longer, has also been more intensely hostile.

Table IV indicates a significant correlation between time and performance, particularly at the farther end of the time scale. In the two tribal groups of which we have the largest sample, the five Kiowa families' and the six Sioux families' position on the scale corresponds directly with the length of time in the area. We might conclude that the longer families stay the better they do—or the better they do the longer they stay; probably both interpretations have validity. Those who do not do well on relocation are "washed out" and go back. Also time in the area allows for the gradual accumulation of better things, the gradual working out of domestic processes. None of the families in the relatively comfortable circumstances represented by Group IV and Group V have been here less than four years, and two of the three families in the highest group have been here more than twenty years.

Table V places emphasis on the wife as the homemaker and compares her success with her education. Here the diagonal of correlation is clear at the lower end of the education scale but not at the top. No education as with the Pomo wives, or very little education as with the Eskimo wives, is clearly associated with the lowest groupings. But whether a greater education is enough to raise the level to the higher groups appears to depend on other factors.

Table VI shows how the families are grouped in relation to income level based on approximate figures projected from hourly or weekly wages. Here again the diagnoal of correlation which might be expected is fairly clear. It becomes even clearer when the size and composition of the family are weighed in. The families to the left of the diagnoal are the smallest, while those to the right of it are the largest.

Sifting the Data into a Structured Conclusion

We have examined the mass of data that can be transcribed from records of habitations, and we have suggested the sorts of correlations that can be made be-

TABLE VI

INCOME LEVEL COMPARED WITH QUALITY AND CONDITION OF FURNISHINGS

		INCOME LEVEL			
		$3000–$3999	$4000–$4999	$5000–$6999	$7000–$8999	$9000 and up
QUALITY AND CONDITION OF FURNISHINGS	I		Pomo I[4]	Pomo II[4]		
	II		Eskimo II[1] Eskimo I[2]	Navajo-Hualapai[4] Sioux I[1,5] Sioux II[3] Sioux III[4]		
	III	Kiowa I[1] Kiowa-Eskimo[1]	Kiowa III[1]		Navajo[3]	
	IV			Kiowa-Choctaw[2,5]	Miwok[4] Sioux V[2] Basque-Rincon[2]	Sioux IV[2,5]
	V					Italian-Seminole[2]

Notes:

Figures not available for Laguna and Kiowa II.

Chippewa-Tutunai and Sioux VI, both retired, are omitted as not comparable.

[1] Families with one to three children under five.

[2] Families with one to three children including some over five.

[3] Families with four children under ten.

[4] Families with four or more children including teen-agers.

[5] Households including a third adult.

tween these details and the details of data from other sources. To go further than this, the assignment must weave into designs that allow for the recognition of more complex significance. This requires that the data be funneled into structures so that further relationships can be grasped. A scientific frame of reference had to be created or this compounding could never take place.

Based on the evidence of the whole study and our empirical experience of making the photographs, we structured our households around five models of adjustment and two models of failure. James Hirabayashi, the project director, referred to these models as "coping cultures." This process allowed our material to relate directly to the project as a whole and gave us distinctive points of observation.

The "Look" of a Home and the Indian's Sense of Identification

The "look" of the Indian home shows a significant relation to the way the Indian family is coping with the problems of urban adjustment and identification. Methods of coping, as evidenced in the study of the data in the photographs, and interpreted with the insights of interview material and direct observation, can be thought of in terms of positive and negative accomplishments: The Indian succeeds by his system, or exhibits one or another degree of stress, or leaves and goes home.

Two basic negative systems appear in our sample, where, by both material and emotional achievement, the Indians seem to be in the process of failing or, to one degree or another, have "failed" on relocation.

(1) A resignation that *native culture has been left behind* and, therefore, there is no purpose in continuing Indian or Eskimo ties, *yet* at the same time there is *no satisfaction in establishing white associations.* The result is a lack of identity with either culture, so that life is carried on in a vacuum.

(2) An *inability to handle white urban values* due to inadequacy of basic education or cultural language. Ties with tribe and Indian relatives may be warm and relations with white people open and hospitable. Yet living on a level of such poverty and deprivation in a city can become unbearable because the development of a secure and satisfying life appears impossible. The hallmark of this ineptitude is extreme disorganization.

There appear to be five systems that make living on relocation tolerable:

(1) An adjustment based on the understanding that relocation is a pragmatic economic opportunity, as off-reservation wage work always has been, not necessarily permanent settlement·in the urban area. Contact with the home reservation is maintained. Prospering here may be a means of gaining prestige; experience and money both can be taken back. *You can go home.*

(2) An effort to make life on relocation satisfying by continuing or even intensifying social and cultural *interaction with Indians of the same or closely related tribes in the urban area.*

(3) An effort to preserve identity by social and even political *interaction with Indians in general.* This may involve advertising the worth of being Indian by open hospitality to white friends.

(4) An effort to become an *individual* in the white society, neither rejecting "Indianness" and Indian ties, nor particularly attempting a compulsive white-urban conformity or seeking out white friends. This exploits the atmosphere of acceptance of cultural diversity possible in a metropolitan atmosphere.

(5) A *turning away from Indian identity* and a compulsive effort to join the white urban society with the intent of never leaving it. This adjustment approaches total assimilation.

Table VII presents these coping systems schematically, according to the ranking of the families by quality and condition of furnishings as seen from the photographs. The five groups used are the same as in Table I. The patterns in this

TABLE VII

Coping Culture Systems: Attitudes toward Indian Identification

			NEGATIVE SYSTEMS		FUNCTIONING SYSTEMS				
			No ties to either culture	Cultur- ally inept	Can go home	Tribal group here	Pan- Indian	Individ- ual	Tribal ties cut
	I	Pomo I		x	x	x			
		Pomo II		x	x	x			
		Eskimo II	x						
		Eskimo I				x			
		Hualapai-							
	II	Navajo		x	x				
		Sioux I			x	x			
		Sioux II			x	x			
		Sioux III			x	x			
		Laguna			x	x			
		Navajo			x	x	x		
		Kiowa I			x	x			
	III	Kiowa II			x	x			
		Kiowa III			x	x			
		Kiowa-Eskimo						x	
		Miwok				x		x	
		Kiowa-Choctaw				x			
	IV	Sioux IV				x			
		Sioux V				x	x		
		Basque-Rincon				x		x	
		Italian-Seminole							x
	V	Chippewa- Tutunai							x
		Sioux VI			x	x			

QUALITY AND CONDITION OF FURNISHINGS

chart will be cleared when we describe individual households in the following pages. We may say in summary:

(a) The negative systems are understandably associated with low ratings.

(b) The possibility of returning home may be more important to those who are not yet functioning as well as they might like in the urban setting.

(c) Tribal group identification in the city appears mportant to all groups to which it is available.

(d) Pan-Indianism can be seen as an additional or alternative support.

(e) Individualism as reflected by personal expression in home decor emerges as a system for dealing positively with urban living. It is associated with a fairly high ranking in this sample, and does not necessarily indicate a lack of Indian identification.

The alternative of cutting off Indian ties is associated with the highest group in the sample, but is represented in the table only by tribal groups for whom there is very little opportunity for association in the Bay Area. The special case of Sioux VI is reported in detail below.

Systems of Failure

(1) LACK OF FUNCTIONING TIES WITH EITHER NATIVE OR WHITE CULTURE   The most basic reason for the failure of relocation comes from a resignation that Indian native culture has been left behind, and that there is no purpose in continuing to maintain Indian ties. When this is matched by an equally hopeless view of human achievement in the surrounding white world, there is no satisfaction gained from white ties either. The result is that life is lived in a vacuum with no self-supporting identification and few expressions of life satisfaction of any kind other than alcohol.

The Eskimo II Family

Observations from the photos: The barest home in the sample. Almost no artifacts on walls or shelves that show local association, or any association, except calendars, newspapers, and television. Beyond the mechanical means of survival the home has nothing except a television set, a plastic airplane cockpit toy, and a table to sit around in a warm neat kitchen. Though old, the house looks reasonably clean and in order, except for the usual tangle of small bedrooms lived in by young children.

Comparison with other households: This home ranks third in quality and condition of furnishings in our sample of 22; this places it in Group II, "mostly serviceable but graceless . . ." The actual pieces of furniture are better than those of the Pomo families, though fewer in number. The bareness makes for a sort of order, even formality. On a three point scale the home is rated one for quantity of possessions, two for order, and three for formality.

The most marked characteristic of this Eskimo's home was its emptiness. The family's psychological struggle for survival was evident in the relative cleanliness and order, but visually the house was barren. Nowhere was there a symbol of cultural self-expression, beyond the empty neatness of the house itself. Apparently this total lack of association was a projection of the husband, who had no friends, no associations, and drank alone at home. The wife on the other hand did have strong cultural ties and prides which she kept submerged. When we visited, to the apparent annoyance of the father but to the delight of the three children, the mother opened a trunk and displayed a beautiful fur parka, which she proudly put on for us to photograph. The husband's self-expression was to sit quietly with a mounting sense of tension within himself. His Eskimo world had closed behind him, the white world was closed in front of him.

Reasonably, this cultural isolation might have begun before the Eskimo went on relocation, perhaps during some early displacing circumstances in Alaska. But the stress of life in the big city completed his disorientation, making success on relocation impossible. Eventually this sad man reached a point of emotional illness that required his return to Alaska, at the expense of the Bureau of Indian Affairs.

(2) FAILURE THROUGH CULTURAL INEPTITUDE   Unquestionably the most common reason for failure on relocation comes from a lack of skill in handling white urban ways and values. This might be due to inadequacy in basic education, or failure to master the language of culture needed to get along in the larger society.

Failure of this kind does not mean the Indians have necessarily broken ties with their past, nor does it mean they have failed to make warm ties with individual white people. It means, rather, that they have failed for reasons of utter poverty or vocational and technological inability, to function effectively in the urban environment. This places the Indian relocation failure alongside the common failure of the larger image of poverty. Of the three Indian families in our sample which can be considered in this inadequately functioning category, a Pomo I family can serve as our model.

The Pomo I Family

Observations from the photos: This home contains plenty of things, yet presents a real image of poverty. The living room, that also serves as a bedroom, has large dilapidated sofas and easy chairs, two television sets, and miscellaneous items, some placed with care as valued objects, others strewn about. The kitchen, lit by a bare light bulb, shows the standard appliances—refrigerator, enameled stove, sink. Clean dishes are in the drain, a box of oatmeal is placed by the stove for breakfast, food goods are pushed back on the open cupboard shelves. The single window opens on a court. The walls are stained and damaged.

Photos of the family with visitors (related) from next door, show a relaxed, laughing, fun-loving group, seemingly in good health and without a care in the world.

Comparison with other households: This home ranks 1, the lowest of our 22 households in regard to quality and condition of furnishings. This places them of course in Group I, characterized as "mostly serviceable but graceless, utility more important than style." On a three-point scale it is rated 2 for quantity of possessions, and 1 for order and formality.

The inventory of the Pomo I home reflects real poverty in the very limited value of the artifacts visible in the home. The failure of the Pomo wife, who has had no schooling at all, to achieve the vocational skill necessary for living in the urban area is expressed, directly, through the ineptitudes of domesticity. The chaos of objects thrown together with some elements of fluent nativistic self-expression, reveal an inability to bring the white world into focus, or to select out of it anything of true satisfaction or status.

Systems of Success

(1) PRAGMATIC UNDERSTANDING THAT YOU CAN GO HOME AGAIN   This first functioning system may be buried in most Indian relocation, the reality that you *can* go home again—not only that the reservation represents refuge if you fail, but that you can succeed well in the white world and then retire back into your native Indian environment as a successful educated individual. In some cases the migrant leaves home with the intention of returning well in mind, works tranquilly on relocation, saves his money, gets an on-the-job education, and then in one to five years returns to pick up his life on the reservation. For others the desire to return home after succeeding in relocation is an emerging concept—an increasing desire and an economic possibility as an Indian reaches retirement. The two approaches may be reflected quite differently in the home. Indians who are short term visitors to urban society with a strong belief that they will go home again within a year or five years, have homes that are singularly empty and sometimes present a hotel room environment, while those who arrive at this understanding through emerging experience of a number of years, even 20 years, in the urban white world may fill their homes with status symbols of white society and show considerable effort and adaptive skill in dealing with white culture.

The Laguna Family

Observation from photos: The large living room is divided in function, sofa and easy chair oriented toward the television at one end, the other end serving as dining and workshop space with tables, chairs, kitchen type cabinets, and storage of various objects. The kitchen itself, though compact, is modern and in immaculate order. There are two double beds in one bedroom, a double bed and crib in another. There is an embroidered bureau scarf on the back of the sofa, a Pendleton blanket on the back of the chair. Since the sofa is pulled out from the wall, it shows that a reupholstery job failed to cover the original material, a large-figured tapestry of a Persian scene, while the new material is mottled and nondescript. Piling of objects on the cabinet in the dining room and storage cartons in the bedroom, and the children doing homework on the kitchen table suggest that the family, with four children from three to sixteen, might be crowded in this four room home.

Comparison with other households: The home ranks 9th in our sample of 22 in quality and condition of furnishings. This is in the middle group, Group III

(Reasonably good, nothing basic lacking, frugal, modest, but selective.) In the three categories of quantity of possessions, order and formality it ranks two, or average, on the three-point scale. In style it was very much in keeping with Pueblo domesticity, well-ordered, clean, furniture sturdy, nothing fancy.

This Pueblo family appeared to have made a successful adjustment to life in the Bay Area. Although there were four growing children and only two bedrooms, the home did not seem crowded, possibly because it was relatively empty. It showed little accumulation of status symbols. Large areas of wall space were bare and the only major decoration in the home was the "shrine" area centered around the mantle of a dummy fireplace and a large photograph of an airplane carrier on which he had served as a young man in World War II. Centered in front of this print was a trophy he had won in local Indian sports competition. Flanking the mantle and the picture on the barren wall on each side of this display hung carefully arranged kachina dolls draped with Indian dance sashes. It must be noted that Pueblo Indian home interiors tend to be sparsely decorated and open; yet it is realistic to consider that the emptiness of this home, void of collected status symbols of our culture, is an expression of a transient position on relocation.

(2) IDENTIFICATION WITH MEMBERS OF SAME TRIBAL GROUP ALSO IN THE URBAN AREA   The second system of coping culture seems to be a significant means of achieving successful relocation, whether it be from Appalachia or from the Navajo Reservation. This has been a successful process among the San Francisco Chinese for two or three generations. Here a transplanted culture of foods, work roles, social interaction, and language have allowed incoming Chinese immigrants to function as a group essentially insulated from the American society, therefore escaping many of the rigors of readjustment.

The system has equal relevance in the problem of urban cross-cultural adjustments among minorities such as the Mexican-Americans, Latin Americans, Puerto Ricans, Cubans, and Negroes. These various transplanted ethnic groups suffer similar difficulties in exercising their personalities and intelligence effectively in the going system of the dominant American culture, which has no ready place for their particular kinds of self-expression, integrity, and productivity. A crisis is met in the first contact, which too often throttles the system of values that allows even a fractured cultural group to function. If this condition persists and a new system is not internalized from the greater society people become displaced, even more ineffectual, and often hostile. In effect, such displaced people fall in the chasm between two cultures—unable to continue the one left behind, unable to afford the one that lies ahead. In Indian relocation one popular adjustment process that appears to appreciably reduce both anxiety and anomie is an effort to make life satisfying by continuing or even intensifying the Indian culture of the relocatee, by a readaptation of native values directly into the new urban setting. This system tends to restrict a family's cultural movement to their own tribal group and may set up large barriers between them and the white world at large where no appreciable interaction takes place. But in a sense this may be an initial phase of learning to operate with an Indian identity in a white world.

The Kiowa-Choctaw Family

Observations from photos: This house has a sizeable living room-dining room combination, ample bedrooms, and an efficient kitchen. At the living room end, the fireplace and television are side-by-side as the focus for a self-contained square of two sofas against either wall and an upholstered chair matching one of the sofas. The dining end has a long formica-topped table, matching chairs, and a desk. The kitchen is thoroughly equipped with appliances, built-in cupboards, adequate though cluttered workspace. The wife is ironing in a bedroom furnished with large matching suite, double bed, chest, dressing table.

Indian-oriented decorations set a dominant tone throughout the house, particularly in the living room where pictures and souvenir banners from trips back to Oklahoma are hanging over the fireplace. Indian art includes reproductions of Bodmer paintings and a modern silk-screen print by an Oklahoma Indian artist.

During the photographic visit the family brought out and exhibited dance costumes, a book of historical Kiowa leaders, and played Kiowa music from a stack of records. In the kitchen the wife made Kiowa fried bread, which was served to all.

Comparison with other households: This house ranks sixteenth in the sample of 22 families in quality and condition of furnishings, in Group IV, the next-to-highest group, characterized as "generally well furnished, ample; an eye to comfort and hospitality; not too particular about style, but some flair." On a three point scale it ranked three for quantity of possession, two for order, and ones for formality. In style the house is personal, unpretentious, comfortable and hospitable, though somewhat crowded. The display of Indian material is the largest in sample.

The house had an air which seemed to speak, "Yes, we've mastered the urban culture, but we're going on being Kiowas." Though there was no resistance to the urban technology, neither was there any display of the status symbols of the urban world. Though the family had lived six years in a respectable sub-division, they said they had made no contacts, even with their next door neighbors. Though the husband is a Choctaw, he related his social life to Kiowa activities. The mother and children were completely absorbed with Kiowa history, music, dances, and social activity in the Bay Area. Their social life is with Indians, particularly in the south end of the Bay Area and centers in the regular Indian activities and "Pow-Wows" in San Jose. The essence of this positive spirit of continued tribal identity was expressed by the wife, "San Jose is a great place for the Kiowa people!"

(3) PAN-INDIAN IDENTIFICATION   An evolutionary movement of the nativistic process occurs when the Indian relocatee begins to identify himself with the Indian culture of America at large outside of his tribal group. This third system places the Indian in an international role in the urban culture, comparable to being an Oriental or an African, and makes use of his ethnic base as a foundation for relating to other groups and for public acceptance. This approach to nativism does not necessarily isolate the Indian either within his tribal group or even within the Indian population. Relocatees who succeed in this effort consider themselves public ambassadors of the Indian world to the white world. They may have large white associa-

tions and offer hospitality not only to Indians of their own tribe but to Indians of all tribes and to white people who are sympathetic to the Indian identity. Possibly, this is an important accomplishment within the relocation process. It allows Indians to function independently but cooperatively in the white urban world, brings to bear all the efficiency of their personality and the support of their cultural identity, and appears to make them more effective individuals.

The Sioux V Family

Observation from photos: House has a fairly large living room, two sofas and easy chair in good condition, free-form coffee table, two odd step-tables, large television console, and at the dining end a formica topped dinette table with matching chairs, and a piano. Kitchen small but efficient, with built-in sink, tiled work counters, ample cupboards, good-size stove, large refrigerator, water heater, utensils in view, moderate priced in good condition. Bedrooms not photographed. No books in living room, but government publication on Black Hills brought out for interview. There is a guitar on wall. Various animal figurines, other decorative ceramics, and crystal horses heads are scattered throughout the house, large pictures hang on walls, including very large photo-mural of Pacific Northwest Coast.

Watchtower, a Jehovah's Witnesses' give-away magazine, is the only Christian item. The only Indian items are a small beaded rosette hung up with the guitar, an archery set (fiber-glass) demonstrated in the back yard, and also in back yard two white wall tents set up to store possessions of various Sioux friends.

Comparison with other households: Ranks 18th in sample of 22 in quality and condition of furnishings, in Group IV (next-to-highest), same group as Kiowa-Choctaw. In all three categories of quantity of possessions, order, and formality, the home ranked two on the three point scale. As these ratings would suggest, the home was open, comfortably relaxed, uncluttered, reflecting a general value system of midwestern hospitality, casually modern in style.

Interview material indicates this Sioux, a highly paid painter for a contracting company, is a dominant leader politically in both Sioux and Pan-Indian activities in the Bay Area. His Pan-Indianism seems to provide him the public role of an Indian in the larger society. An attractive daughter has married a white man, who is now very much part of the family, and who also practices archery. The home appeared to have an open door to the surrounding white neighborhood as well. The cultural inventory shows considerably less concern for Indian symbols than the Kiowa-Choctaw home; yet social and intellectual expression constantly involves the destiny of Indians, with strong overtones of Pan-Indianism, where Indians can operate on an equal footing in the larger white society. The air of the home is as relaxed as the Kiowa-Choctaw home. It is the relaxation of a family that appeared to us to meet the dominant urban culture on its own terms, interacting with it freely but sustaining a powerfully mobilized identity of being Sioux *and* American Indians.

(4) MAKING AN INDIVIDUAL ROLE   The fourth adjustment is one by which a relocated Indian can live at peace in urban society without compulsive anxiety about

being or not being an Indian, making his way based entirely upon himself as an individual, but not necessarily a conforming individual. Success in this endeavor seems involved in not rejecting "Indianness," because this is apt to throw one into a compulsive white conformity that would destroy the relaxed nature of this success and invite a sense of inferiority. We might call this the emerging worldly Indian individual in the urban society. The Indian could compare himself to a worldly Frenchman, in the larger society who reasonably needs emotional support from his background at various points and does not deny it, but sees the need in larger perspective.

One young family in our sample which is adjusting to relocation in this way, is made up of an Eskimo student, his wife, a Kiowa girl from Kansas, and their eight-month-old son.

The Kiowa-Eskimo Family

Observations from photos: A large high-ceiling living room and bedroom, with a kitchen area built into a partitioned end of the living room. The rooms are sparsely and selectively furnished, small couch covered with a Pendleton, a Danish-modern type easy chair, a basket chair, modern step bookcase, and portable television in the living room. Japanese dolls are placed on the bookcase, Orozco and Utrillo prints are on the wall, and subdued indirect lighting gives the impression of "sophisticated" image. The kitchen has a very large refrigerator, compact but new appliances, well designed shelf-space. There is a double bed with a good chenille spread, a chest with an elaborate collection of baby care items, a baby's car bed, and much empty space in the bedroom.

Comparison with other households: In quality and condition of furnishings this household ranked 14th of the 22, the highest in Group III (the middle group, "reasonably good, nothing basic lacking, frugal, modest, but selective"). On a three point scale it rated two in quantity of possessions, three in order, and two on formality. The home was decorated with care and restraint. The young couple were outgoing and so was the home, with an air hospitable to change and influence.

The arrangement and decor of the Kiowa-Eskimo home express great efforts at personal taste. A diverse artistic and dramatic flair is apparent with Utrillo and Orozco reproductions and a shrine area of Japanese dolls and trinkets. It is not until one enters the bedroom that it is evident you are in an Indian home. Here is a mantle decorated with snapshots from the wife's Kiowa background, Indians in costume and scenes of native life surrounding her family.

The home shows a strong desire to rise above conformity and conventional status symbols. There are no nativistic symbols, other than the snapshots of the Kiowa wife's family. Probably this young couple exhibits an ideal accomplishment of relocation, devoid of serious compulsions or rejections, or a flattening conformity to urban middle class tastes.

(5) TURNING AWAY FROM INDIAN IDENTITY This system of relocation approximates, by and large, the goals of both the Indian Service and the missionary

organizations in their efforts to assist the Indians in adjusting to the modern white world, based on a belief that they should reject their Indian background completely "for their own good," reject their past with a compulsion and even a revulsion.

A variation of this fifth system, which might be called an example of success by involuntary rejection of Indian personality, is the scheme of a retired couple, a Tutunai (from the Oregon Coast) married to a Chippewa. The Tutunai has retired from an industrial job, but *has* no people to return to even if he wanted to, for his tribal group has practically disappeared. His wife was an orphan raised by missionaries away from her culture, so there is no culture for her to return to either. Hence involuntarily this couple have had to succeed by the fifth system of survival, completely separated from any nativistic support. The couple did not turn away from their past with revulsion, but simply—they felt their past was dead.

The Chippewa-Tutunai Family

Observations from the photos: Fairly large living room-dining room combination. Matching sofa and easy chair, large relaxizer chair, two occasional chairs, coffee table, step table, other small table, telephone stand, television, radio-phonograph console. Almost every table and shelf surface is covered with hand-crocheted doilies, sofa with hand-crocheted wool afghan, easy chair covered with blanket, wall-to-wall carpeting covered with small throw rugs in front of large chairs. Kitchen small, built-in sink, cupboards, tiled counter (less counter space than many other homes), rather old but originally expensive combination gas range-trash burner, large refrigerator. Ironing board folds down from built-in closet. Electric coffee maker, osterizer, mixer, toaster, waffle iron. Dishes and utensils visible all of good quality. Garage holds automatic washer, water heater, electric roaster, ten gallon crock, shelves of canned goods, piles of cartons. Master bedroom has double bed with headboard, covered with hob-nail spread, satin throw pillows, matching suite of two large dressers. Second bedroom has a large bed too with hob-nail spread, dressing table matching the other dressers. Beside the crocheted handiwork, the house is decorated chiefly with flowers and plants, by nicknacks, mostly ceramic figurines, decorative plates on the mantle above the unused fireplace, cards, and photographs. Books include the *Encyclopaedia Britannica* and a few others.

Single Christian symbol is white ceramic figure of Christ. There is one small figurine of an Indian on horseback, and one blanket which looks as though it were a Pendleton.

Comparisons with other households: This house, the most thoroughly furnished in the sample, is ranked 21st of the 22 in quality and condition of furnishings, surpassed only by Sioux VI which strikes a somewhat higher level of elegance. It is one of the three houses in the highest Group V, differing sharply from the casual (yet really very comfortable) homes in Group IV, (such as Kiowa-Choctaw or Sioux V) in its essential fussiness, as well as the high consistency of the good quality of objects accumulated over the years. On a three point scale it is rated three for all three categories of quantity of possessions, order, and formality. (It must be remembered this is a comparative rating for these homes; this is still an unpretentious, hospitable home.)

The home of this couple presents a vivid look of how they have mastered their urban white circumstances. Their home is a fortress of internal effort and material security. The house is the most congested and over-furnished abode in our sample, but with all its effort the environment appears one of social isolation. No doubt, all around them are countless other retired couples faced with the problem of socialization in the later years, but many of them are settling back into family, the warmth of their own backgrounds and interacting with other like couples who share similar sentiments. The question raised is, where is the cultural support of this Indian couple coming from in their declining years? The visual impression of isolation is heightened by the considerable storage of goods in the house, with food, tools, and even vats of water ostensibly stored to comply with recommendations from Civil Defense. To be sure, they have given up keeping a car and have to shop ahead, but the amount of goods and equipment stored all through the house gives the appearance that they were surviving in a modern wilderness of white culture.

Completing the Circle

We have just looked at a family which represents success achieved by severing Indian ties and assimilating the dominant culture's value system. Their comparative success in this effort is shown by their ranking of 21st in our sample in quality and condition of furnishings. Yet what of the family that ranks 22nd?

This is the Sioux VI couple, who have lived for 20 years in the Bay Area and recently retired. They own a small home in a comfortable community, which conforms well to the husband's statement of how to get along: "You have to keep your lawns well trimmed and your fences painted to make it in the white world." In spite of their obvious sucess by white standards, they have decided to return to their Sioux country and their Sioux people.

The interior of the house seems to speak, "We've mastered the white world. We've got the best." But also the impersonality of this mastery makes it possible to add, "Now we are ready to leave." Every detail conforms to the standards of the middle class home. The living room is in excellent matching taste with subdued lighting; the kitchen super-efficient, cheerful and well lit; the bedrooms expansive and well furnished. Yet when we visited, the husband's self-expression was to bring out a Sioux wooden flute adorned with an eagle feather, which he played for us with pride. The impressive image is that they have conquered our status system and are now ready to move out and return to American Indian culture. They are planning to visit a sister in an Indian hospital bordering the Navajo and then return to the husband's home in North Dakota.

Should the Sioux VI couple's system of coping be counted as in the first "You can go home again" group? They have "assimilated" the dominant culture's value system very well indeed, as have those who have successfully cut themselves off from their Indianness, yet the Sioux VI couple have never lost contact, have gone back to the Dakotas over the years, and are at present much concerned about a religious controversy on the reservation. Probably the decision to return was arrived at by a growing awareness over the years and was crystallized since the husband's retirement. Surely it depended on the fact that the Sioux people, though harassed with problems, are still there, still a center of vitality, something to go back to.

The Potential of Visual Analysis

Unquestionably, the inventory approach is both a stabilizer of content and a door into the treasure of photographic data. The first step in any research with photographs should be an open-ended appraisal of all the nonverbal elements; if they are left obscured within the complexity of the realism they represent, we may never recognize the wealth of our evidence.

After the fieldwork, what have you found? Certainly before we think in terms of conclusions, we need to weigh the gross sum of evidence, counting the smallest items, for at this stage how can we know what the missing piece of the puzzle might be?

As we have demonstrated, the basic methodology of counting, evaluating, and comparing of photographic content leads to very complex analysis. This approach is consistent with scientific processes. With it we can arrive at a sound position for appraising the cyclopedic mass of documentation found within cultural photographs. Elements that might remain intangible can be anchored into a cultural frame that can finally accommodate the whole photographic record.

9

Technical Problems of Research Photography

How GOOD A technician do you have to be to use the camera for research? And how professional does your equipment have to be? There is basic data available for every level of photographic skill, from the novice with the box camera to the perfectionist with an 8- by 10-in. view camera or a multi-lens Leica. The skilled cameraman certainly can glean data that is out of reach of the learning amateur, yet there remain very important observations that can be made with the amateurishly operated snapshot camera. Some varieties of sociometric tracking can be done as well with the box camera as with the professional camera of the same negative size. Extreme sharpness is not essential in counting riders at a street car stop, or school children milling around in the play yard. Simple counting and rudimentary identification can be made from very unskillful records.

Camera skill does *not* insure gathering readable data. The expert observer could gather more significant material with the box camera than the visually blind super-technician with a five hundred dollar camera. The challenge is *to observe with scientific significance.* With this view, rudimentary technique and an adequate camera are all any anthropological student needs.

The relatively greater significance of visual awareness as compared with technical skill was demonstrated by a group photographic study made by two anthropologist couples, the Cohns and the Planalps, working for their doctorates in a small village near Banaras, India. This was on one of the Cornell Community Study Programs, others being carried out in Japan, Thailand, Nova Scotia and on the Navajo Reservation in the American Southwest. Bernard S. Cohn, now Associate Professor of Anthropology and History at the University of Chicago, and Shirley Planalap, now with the University of Oregon, decided a few weeks before enplaning for India to use photography for enthnographic recording. Neither had done photography before or owned anything more than a snapshot camera. To meet their needs, serviceable 2¼- by-2¼-in. twin-lens reflex cameras and light meters were ordered, and the team had time left for just four exercises in basic camera technique.

My first stipulation was that they write down all the technical data for each exposure in the four short lessons so that they could learn completely from the examples of each developed roll of film. This is a most important procedure in mastering technique rapidly. Taking a few rolls of film systematically and writing down the exposures can teach anyone the rudiments in a few days of study.

The first lesson was how to expose film with the aid of the light meter. The students were cautioned that they could expect their meters to break or deteriorate in tropical field conditions, and, when they arrived in India, to make careful light studies of all recording conditions, writing the data down for future reference. The students carefully exposed film, noting meter readings and camera settings, working light values through from bright landscapes to deep shade and home interiors.

We developed the film together in the Cornell lab so that they would have a follow through view of the process, and see at once their successes and mistakes.

The second lesson was in controlling the focus of the lens by working through from infinity to three foot close-ups. The third lesson was photographing a model carrying through a process, making each step visually clear. The fourth lesson was photographing artifacts, using natural light to sharpen detail, and the camera ground glass for sharp focus and sensible framing.

Dr. Cohn's recall of this crash training highlights what probably is most important in the orientation of the anthropologist who goes to the field with a camera.

The points I remember about the experience were:

(1) Your ability to relax me regarding the technical aspects of photography by driving home the relative simplicity, especially with a reflex camera, of the operation.

(2) Your insistence that one should see the picture before one took it rather than hope for the best.

(3) The necessity to take a lot of pictures and in sequence.

(4) Your 'eye' in seeing how a picture would look when enlarged or cropped.[1]

Our lessons stopped here. They were urged not to process their own film, though they carried equipment to do so, except for emergency checking of their field results. Instead it was suggested that they find a reliable film processor in Baharas, give him several rolls of film shot at a variety of film speeds, check for the best exposure, note the film rating and expose everything at that speed for the whole film period, being very careful always to have the same man develop the film as nearly as possible in the same way.

Their supplementary camera equipment included K-2 filters for screening out the white glare of dusty tropical skies, light tripods for careful close-ups, lens tissue and dust off brushes. The cameras were in ever-ready cases, with instructions to keep these cases closed at all times except when working, for *dust* is the wrecker of cameras. They were instructed to store their film in *cool places,* with bulk storage of film in iceboxes whenever possible. This is particularly important after film has been exposed. Film deteriorates rapidly once removed from its packing and exposed to the light. *This is especially true of color film.* Heat and moisture can ruin this sensitive emulsion altogether.

---

[1] Private communication.

I did not see this field team for a year and a half. I was full of anxiety and anticipation, for in letters they had reported a very exhaustive film coverage. When I saw their 1000 contact prints I was both heartened and amazed. Despite their limited instructions the team returned with an outstanding visual ethnography.

Various elements had worked for their success. The even brilliance of their negatives was the result of good synchronization between exposing and processing and their regularity of getting their film to the lab in Banaras quickly so that they avoided the general fogging that is the hazard of film deterioration in hot countries. Another element was their good judgment not to force the lighting conditions. Recording was done whenever possible in the stable light hours of the day.

Still another basis of their success was thoughtful planning. Shirley Planalp and Rella Cohn concentrated on the women's world within the home compounds, where few men are allowed to go, while Bernard Cohn and Jack Planalp worked solely in the men's world. Having cameras in both these domains greatly enriched the research files. But beyond these technical points we must credit their success to their excellent training in cultural significance of circumstance and artifact, that they had received from Dr. Morris Opler in the year preceding their expedition in the field. As noted earlier in this writing, Opler had bombarded his students with the photographed roles of Indian society in the region where the study was made. The students' training in significance was unquestionably the key to their success, for it gave them sharp recognition and triggered heir cameras at the right moment.

In an effort to carry this thoughtful study through to its visual conclusion, the Cohns and Planalps made a generous selection of their more important negatives, and we shipped the negatives to COMPO, one of the finest professional photographic laboratories in New York where many magazine photo-essayists have their work processed. The lab returned 8- by 10-in. prints and to the satisfaction of the photographers, the technical and visual content of their study could match any professional study made in India. It is apparent that the eye makes the picture. Fine photography is fine observation.

Some Critical Factors

What *is* a good ethnographic photograph beyond its specialized content of data? Good technique does extend the readability of a photograph. As an example, in refined studies of cultural inventories a soft focus negative is of little value—for precise reading it is impossible.

Critical image involves three factors: the nature of the lens, lack of camera movement, and proper adjustment of the point of optical focus. If you are paying $100 for a camera you should check out the lens. Even costly lenses can be defective, for the sharpness of a lens depends as much upon how its elements are mounted as on the optical formulae. Always examine *with a magnifying glass* the back surface of your lens. *The slightest marring on the back surface makes the lens soft focus.* So will fungus between the elements of the lens. Fungus appears almost like etching on the surface of the elements. Scratches on the front of the lens are of negligible importance. *See that all elements are screwed together tightly.* The slightest movement of elements will change the focus of a lens.

Check your lens by making two tests. Photograph a newspaper with black type at the closest point of camera focus with the lens aperture wide open, and then again stopped down. Make a second test at infinity, ideally showing sharp building lines, signs, or electric wires. Again expose film with the lens wide open, and then stopped down. The results of these tests will tell you whether or not your lens is flat field and sharp to the edges. They will tell you whether your lens is critically sharp wide open, and your view of infinity will check out the resolving power of your lens. Infinity is the extreme test of a lens. Spy-in-the-sky cameras can resolve measurements of one foot taken at fifteen miles.

If you have a good lens and still get soft focus, study how you hold your camera. Make tests and *find out how slow a shutter speed you can hold without blur.* The calm individual can make a sharp negative easily at a twenty-fifth and even a tenth of a second. The nervous type can't hold an exposure slower than $\frac{1}{50}$th. If this is a problem, lean against a wall when you shoot necessarily slow exposures in very dim light, or use a tripod. Photographing motion requires a fast shutter. You can stop a running horse at $\frac{1}{500}$th, and craft processes ideally at $\frac{1}{100}$th of a second.

If you get blur with a fast shutter speed, check on your footage scale and the working of your range finder. Range finders can jar and give you a false plane of focus, instead of a focused 5 feet the camera may actually be focusing at 10 feet. To check your focus and test the accuracy of footage scale and range finder, put your camera on a tripod, open the camera, place a strip of wax or tissue paper in place of the film, throw a dark cloth over your head and the back of the camera, and examine the exact point of sharpness through the lens. The image will be accurately reflected on the wax or tissue paper.

Sensible framing of the camera image is a second skill that adds considerably to the research value of a photograph. Framing means adequate coverage. Counting and measuring is not possible if the whole view is not available for study. See that all of the research subject is covered. If this is impossible in one frame, mount together as many frames as necessary to obtain a complete record. The whole view is the scientific view, the composition that gets the most relationships and dimensions. In large operations such as sawmills or shipyards, you want to make very wide view exposures so that all the complex relationships of the industry can be studied. The wide view is equally important for tracking the positions of the workers, ideally to see them in their various roles through the changing phases of manufacture. Hence a wide-angle lens is a practical necessity.

Of all your lens equipment, you will probably find your wide-angle lens is your most valuable. Many anthropologists use wide angle equipment exclusively. To be sure, the telephoto lens offers still another refinement of study. On occasion the sociometric study benefits greatly by the long lens but in general it will not be as valuable as your wide angle. You can always enlarge up a part of a sharp frame, but there is no way of stretching the borders of a confining negative.

Proper timing of photographs also adds to their research value. As in all photography, the anthropologist is a hunter who raises his camera at the right instant, at the most clarifying part of the process, or at the peak of nonverbal expression of the human subject. There is no formula for this success; rather it is a clarity that comes to the photographer through practice and astute observation.

Beyond these technical achievements, fine photography for anthropology is as much the result of good human relations as it is of camera manipulation. An open expressive portrait of the native certainly holds more opportunity for study than a stiff expressionless one; here there is basically a reflection of the relationship between the native and the anthropologist. Photographs that hold intense human significance and communication have often been made by novices with the camera, for the secret of such records lies in the nature of rapport, not in photographic technique.

Cameras for Anthropology

What cameras and lenses get the best results for research. Anthropologists have used every variety of camera for archeological and anthropological recording, from 11- by 14-in. view cameras down to Minox 16 mm "spy cameras." Each specialist seeks his own tools. Historically *all* cameras were view cameras with a ground glass back for full viewing and focusing, and all cameras were large—8 by 10 in., 5 by 7 in., or 4 by 5 in. Little work was enlarged and an ample contact print was a prerequisite of the field record. The truly miniature cameras, the $2\frac{1}{4}$ by $2\frac{1}{4}$ in., and the 35 mm were not in common use till the 1930s. It has only been in the last twenty years that the 35 mm camera has been developed into the all purpose tool that it is today. Modern lenses, improved film and chemicals for processing have made the twin-lens Rolleiflex and its imitators, and the Leica with its competitors, the most widely used cameras in both laboratory and field studies.

Historical archeological records were all done with the 11- by 14-in. or more popular 8- by 10-in. view camera. The large contact print rendered exquisite detail and still remains popular with many eminent archeologists. Paul Martin, Emeritus Curator of Anthropology of the Field Museum of Chicago, commonly logs all his Southwest digs with an 8- by 10-in. camera mounted on a specially constructed movable steel platform ten feet high. We are no longer held to this enormously large film for critical details. Improved lenses allow the 4- by 5-in. camera to offer the archeologist comparable renderings. The issue is no longer sharp images, but rather corrected and carefully framed images. In the field of architectural photography or recording ruins, as in Yucatan, the view camera remains the most professional tool, but 4 by 5 in. instead of the cumbersome 8 by 10 in. The view camera allows for critical correction of distortion due to perspective by its system of tilts, swings, and rising and falling lens adjustments. One drawback to this equipment is that it requires a skilled operator.

Many early records in anthropology were made with a 4- by 5-in. or $3\frac{1}{4}$- by $4\frac{1}{4}$-in. Graflex; though cumbersome its reflex system allowed for critical study of the camera image within seconds of the exposure. This noisy and durable camera is still in use. The viewing mirror snaps up and a cloth shutter with a narrow split races across the film exposing the negatives. This is an excellent tool for photographing native types for physical anthropology. This first "candid" camera has given way to the small twin reflexes and the single lens 35 mm reflexes which, due to their extreme depth of field, accomplish recording of this character as well if not better than the larger equipment.

The 2¼- by 2¼-in. twin-lens reflex is a happy compromise between the large and the very small. Its negative is large enough to allow for comprehensive study, yet the camera is small enough for quick candid recording, and its lens is short enough for a great depth of sharp focus. The full negative-size ground glass allows for precise focusing and adjusting the camera angle so that architecture is not unduly distorted, (when you point your camera up, lines of architecture converge and to correct this fault the camera must be held as nearly level as possible).

Many fieldworkers carry both the twin lens Rolleiflex (or Rolleicord, Mamiyaflex, Ikoflex, and so on) and the 35 mm camera. The amazing 35 mm has many advantages. You can use inexpensive bulk film, the film loads in 36-exposure casettes, the film is edge-numbered. The camera usually has interchangeable lenses, wide angle to telephoto, and its very short lens has a wide aperture that allows for recording in candle light with an adequate depth of field. The reflex 35 mm camera allows for complete viewing on a 35 mm ground glass which means extreme close-ups can be made with precision focusing. Thirty-five millimeter slides are the most popular size for educational slides, and anthropologists—who also invariably teach —often carry the 35 mm loaded with color for precisely this reason. Modern lenses, film, and processing allow the 35 mm to produce very sharp 11- by 14-in. prints. It has become the tool of the professional photo-essayist; most of the pictures in *Life* and *Look* are made with 35 mm cameras.

The 2¼- by 2¼-in. twin-lens reflex cameras—Rolleiflexes, Rolleicords, Yashiflexes—are equipped with standard lenses that are wider-angled than the usual 50 mm focal length lens on the 35 mm camera. But the 35's have the widest angle lenses designed; the 35 mm focal length lens is the most popular of these wide field components. This lens comes in f3.5, and f2.8 in many makes. It is not so wide as to distort the image and makes a fine working lens for the student of technology, social gatherings and regional ecology. Beyond this 35 mm focal length lens there is the "90" and, finally, the latest "fish-eye" lens with a view of 180°. This latter lens *does* distort, but when you are primarily after complete relationships, distortion may not be of significant importance.

One step smaller than the standard 35 mm camera is the half-frame 35, which is literally half the size of the 35 mm. This miniature exposure was first developed for the robot camera that made an exposure automatically every second. It was designed for time and motion studies. In the last few years, many makes of half-frame cameras have come on the market. Professionally they are used in filmstrip production and by cameramen who want the advantage of 72 exposures on a standard 36-frame roll of 35 mm film; the focal length of the lens is even shorter than the standard 35 mm lens and, therefore, has nearly universal focus. With great care in exposure and development, print detail can be gained that compares well with the standard 35 mm camera.

When we move to still smaller cameras, the Minox or the 16 mm Minelota, we can no longer produce professionally clear prints. The 16 mm is one quarter the size of the 35 mm. The contact print is useless for studying, and so far the negative does not produce a critically sharp enlargement. Such a small camera may fill a personal psychological need rather than a realistic documentary one. I am also prejudiced against hiding cameras which is the popular appeal of the Minox. Rarely is it good protocol to work in this way. The main values of the miniature camera are depth of field, speed of operation, and bulk of film. The Minox does not expand these values.

On the other hand, serious observers do use the Minox, including Edward T. Hall. In fact some of the illustrations in *The Hidden Dimension* were made with this tiny camera. Romantically, it is considered a spy camera and would fit nicely up the sleeve of James Bond.

How to Make a Panoramic Study

In the study of homes or in geographic records of communities, the major challenge to the photographer is whole coverage. The research value of photography recedes when we cannot appraise all four sides of a room, or the full sweep of a community. The more elements we *can* relate, count, or qualify, the richer becomes our understanding of the cultural parts.

Use of the wide-angle lens can solve much of this problem. So desirable is this lens that fieldworkers refer to it as "the anthropologist's lens." Getting space photographically, getting whole coverage, becomes the consuming effort.

The standard wide-angle lenses are not wide enough for 180° panoramas, let alone the 360° view which records the complete circle of the landscape. The only way we can obtain such vistas is by multiple exposures, a rough effort which can be accomplished in overlapping shots—from three or four for a 90° sweep to a dozen or more for the full circle. These exposures can be spliced or morticed together in an uninterrupted view of a room or a town, and, if you don't mind optical distortion, the results can be satisfying and a source of dependable information.

The problem is that unless the camera is *perfectly level,* the horizon line will be zig-zagged or curved up and down, when the foreground is accurately morticed. And if the camera does not turn *on the exact axis* of the middle of the lens, foreground and background can never be accurately spliced. The Rolleiflex camera supplies a tilt-top head that makes all these adjustments and allows you to make a perfect 360° view.

Once you have mastered these optical problems, there is the challenge of variable exposure. As you pan from the light-over-your-shoulder to the left or right, or as you pan in a circle directly into the sun, your negative will get increasingly thin in the shadows, and over-exposed in the heavens. To equalize this, you must take light readings for all your camera directions and decide which is more important, perfect skies or readable ground detail.

An exciting way to study a 360° panorama is to enlarge all the frames 8 by 10 in., mount them in a continuous band, fold this strip in a circle *print side in,* suspend this panoramic circle at an eye level, and view the image from *inside*. Every detail will now appear in its natural position.

Problems of Portraiture

The camera has from the start been enthusiastically used to record native types. Despite the great technological advance of photography, early camera records of native people are often superior to the studies made today. The reason for this is a commentary on photographic technique and the art of photography. Two factors, both of which could be thought of as disadvantages actually contributed to this early superiority: the very slow film and the customarily long focal length lenses. Early lenses were little more than pinholes and they had to be of long focal length in order to cover the negative. Wide-angle lenses are the result of modern optical formulas perfected only in recent years. But the long lenses meant that portraits were beautifully corrected. The lenses of Brady's day forced the photographer to be at least six to eight feet from his subject. This meant that noses and ears were rendered in their true proportions. Today if you fill a Rolleiflex ground glass with a portrait head, you must be as close as three feet and the result is that noses and jaws get disastrously distorted, making the records of little use to comparative physical anthropology, as well as unpleasant to look at.

The other factor of success—slow film—challenges the refinements that have gone into making modern film emulsions, sensitive materials that allow us to shoot fast in poor light without the blur of very long exposures. The very slow film of fifty years ago *required* that the camera be used on the tripod, and *required* that the native sit before the lens in a controlled manner, or the image would have been blurred out of all recognition. The inadvertant result of these technological hardships was that portraits were very carefully taken fifty years ago. Ethnic materials were carefully arranged, the native was given the opportunity of composure, and the rapport between the photographer and the subject tended to be more complete than the communication between today's snap-shooter and the surprised Indian.

Of course, there is a compensation in the development of fast film and fast cameras. Now we have the genuinely candid portrait of the native who is oblivious to the photographer. Such records might be essential in recording how a native appears undisturbed in his cultural role, at his work, or in social interaction. But this approach must be clearly separated from just one of snapping pictures of the passing native, where the record too often reflects self-conscious "cheese" grins, bewilderment, or open hostility. Ideally, portraits should be taken with care, and communication between the native and the photographer should be clear. There are many more factors involved in a fine ethnographic portrait than just a framed head. Take your time, and give your subject the opportunity to communicate with the camera.

Distortion that can make records useless to physical anthropology comes from the extreme angle between the lens and the subject when the camera is too close. With wide angle lenses, as found in all $2\frac{1}{4}$- by $2\frac{1}{4}$-in. reflexes, even when a face is recorded at eye level the nose is always distorted, jaws appear protruded, ears appear too small. If you are using a wide-angle lens, *stand back*. The Rolleiflex should not be used closer than *four feet* when an ethnographic portrait is made. Long lenses modify this, because a full portrait head can be framed at six feet or further. An angle shot at six feet has considerably less distortion than the same angle at three feet. Thirty-five millimeter reflex cameras and standard 35s such as the Leica, Contax, and Nikon, all have long lenses that can be used to make well-corrected portraits. The 90 mm focal length lens is beautifully corrected for this purpose.

Through-the-lens reflex cameras invite eye-to-eye portraits which offer maximum correction for the lens used, but *waist level* reflexes are a threat. Portrait after portrait is made with these cameras taken from the belly button, with the eyes of the native staring aimlessly overhead. Actually, he may be looking straight across at *you,* the photographer, but the camera's eye is looking *up.* This can be easily corrected. All waist level reflex cameras have direct view finders that allow you to photograph the subject eye-to-eye. Sometimes, a low angle shot is what you need. But make this a matter of choice, rather than a default of camera technique.

Technology in Action

To blur or not to blur! Many technological circumstances should be sharp. Hands twine fibres, the textile craftsman throws his shuttle through the loom, the farmer drops four kernels of corn in a hole, and fisherman draws a cod from the sea; we can study these techniques clearly if the motion is sharp, without blur that can disguise the way it is done.

Most of the time blur comes becomes the photographer arbitrarily fails to shoot at a shutter speed fast enough to stop the action. But blur can come also from the body movement of the photographer. If light is so poor that you must shoot speeds slower than 1/25th of a second, use a tripod, hold your breath, lean against a wall, or rest your camera on a chair.

It must be remembered, the closer you are to the action the more the blur. You can photograph a horse trotting by 100 feet away at 1/100th of a second, but if you are 10 feet from the trotting horse you need a shutter speed of 1/500th of a second. If action is coming toward you or going directly away from you, a galloping horse can be stopped at 1/100th of a second, whereas if this horse runs across your camera view it would be blurred at 1/500th of a second.

Most crafts should be photographed at 1/100th of a second, but if there is swift action, advance your shutter to 1/250th. If you want to count the kernels of corn dropping in the ground, use 1/250th of a second exposure. If you are photographing a rodeo, use 1/500th or 1/1000th. If you are photographing fishing on the high seas, use 1/500th of a second exposure, or even faster—you can't control the motion of the boat.

Now, should you *always* stop the motion? Paul Ekman, director of the Nonverbal Research Center at Langley Porter Clinic, exploits blur so he can record motion.[2] One camera is used to *stop* motion and get all details sharp, while a sec-

---

[2] Private communication.

ond camera is set at a slow shutter speed to record the presence of motion. One part of the subject's body may be sharp, but the hands or shoulders blurred. By the same technique, a slow shutter speed series on group interaction would reveal *who moved fastest.* Nervous hand gestures would be recorded which might seem insignificant in a frozen-image record.

Photographing with Little Light or No Light

In the Andes at high altitudes, there is little or no light to photograph with under the portals and in the rooms of Indian homes. How can you record? Here you must work with reflected or artificial light. The simplest and most available supplementary light is reflection. Take a five-foot square of white cloth, stretch it on two crossed sticks, and you have a reflector that will flood an Indian's portal with adequate photographic light. If this is too cumbersome, you have three other choices. Within the range of electric circuits you can use photo-flood bulbs; in the field you must either use flash bulbs or strobe light.

Flash bulbs took the place of powder flash, and for three decades most news pictures were made with flash bulbs. These come in a great many varieties and sizes, some as small as peanuts. But each bulb is good for only one shot, and a large supply is bulky to carry, and changing the bulbs every time you take a picture consumes a lot of time. The strobe light, which came into general use in the late 1940s, eliminates the necessity of bulbs. The strobe unit produces an electronic flash of very high level illumination at a very fast speed within a sealed tube. It can be fired again and again with a brief recycling period, thirty seconds to a minute, between shots.

But whether we use flash bulbs or the electronic strobe flash, there are two elements to be considered—enough light, and the right kind of light. When the flash gun is right on the camera it is called flat flash, simply because the flash eliminates all shadows. This is fine for investigating murders, but not very revealing in photographing technology. Without shadows we lose all drawing, all sculptural detail and delineation of planes. Also, as every amateur knows, faces near the camera always appear like floured-faced actors in a minstrel show, whereas people in the near background cannot be seen except as shadows. The only way we can defeat this harshness of lighting is to get the light away from the camera. You can hold the flash reflector in your hand, clamp the light on the wall focusing down at an angle to the subject, or you can flash the light up on the ceiling, if there is one, and *bounce* the light back on the subject. The angle lighting gives hard shadows, but shows good detail in technology. The bounced light gives a more rounded well-modified light over the room area.

How reliable are flash and strobe?

Flash bulbs that go off as the shutter is tripped are synchronized with the shutter and are fired by flash light batteries. If the batteries are weak, no exposure. If the synchronization within the shutter gets faulty, no exposure. Both these failures are very common. In the field you can resort to one sure technique with flash. Open the shutter, fire your flash bulbs or strobe, close the shutter, and you *know*

The author using a strobe light (electronic flash) in a cultural inventory of a Pueblo Indian home in New Mexico.

you have the picture. This is known as "open flash" photography, and is shot with the shutter set at "B," which stands for bulb—the old rubber bulb photographers used to squeeze and release to open and close the shutter.

Strobe guns also are synchronized to the camera shutter and too often the synchronization is at fault. Usually the failure is a loose connection between the camera and the strobe light. If you plan to do a lot of strobe photography it would pay to have a professional strobe connection built into your camera that would insure synchronization. Strobe lights also work on batteries, very powerful ones, but these too can run down and leave you without light. Some strobes can be recharged from a wall socket; they are worth the added investment.

Strobe is far superior to flash bulbs. We used a strobe unit in the Andes for six months before a rain storm shorted the unit. The battery gave us two thousand trouble-free exposures.

Strobe has a rewarding character in that the light is so fast—1/1000th of a second and faster—that people often never really see the light flash. When the strobe is used as a bounce light, it is very hard to detect even in a dimly lighted room, so instantaneous is the light duration.

The answer for all kinds of artificial lighting is to practice using it extensively *before* your expedition. Work the bugs out, learn your technique at home so you can work with confidence in the field.

Photographic Processing in the Field

Should anthropologists develop and print their own material? Modern commercial processing has removed this laborious necessity. Twenty years ago it was extremely difficult to get professionally adequate commercial developing and printing. Today just a few photo-journalists do their own laboratory finishing; the vast majority let trained specialists do it for them.

My advice to the anthropologist in the field would be: develop film *only* when essential, either to avoid deterioration, to check equipment, or to manufacture immediate feedback. Even in this latter case, the Polaroid camera, in most instances, will do the service for you. Even in rural India, Bernard Cohn and Shirley Planalp got excellent results by giving their film to a local processer; though his laboratory was not one to inspire great confidence, he probably did a more dependable job than they could have done in the limitations of their field surroundings.

Nevertheless there are circumstances when processing in the field is essential. On a long field assignment how can you be sure your camera is working properly and whether you are making correct exposures? If you can't get your film to a local processor, then periodically, if possible, you should develop a test roll of film.

To meet this problem the field photographer should carry a compact emergency developing kit: a film tank, thermometer, plastic graduate, and packets of dry chemicals to mix just one tank-full at a time of developer and hypo. Eastman Kodak makes small packets of D-76 and of hypo which are ideal for this purpose; simply follow the directions. Your darkroom is a light-proof bag with elastic-bound sleeves to get your arms inside—a "changing bag." This is an important article for the times when film gets jammed inside a camera, and it also allows you to load your exposed film into the developing tank. The remainder of the process can be carried out in full light. The film you develop as a test should be exposed as a test; do not risk valuable data. After clearing in the hypo bath the test film can be washed briefly in a basin of water and dried for careful inspection. Even lightly washed film will last weeks or even months, so on a water-scarce location you can avoid the laborious problem of washing film for a half-hour.

A second circumstance where a field laboratory could be necessary is on an extended study. Working with your camera records in the field can be of great research value, and sending the film out of the bush or the mountains for processing can be perilous as well as consuming weeks or even months. Setting up a field laboratory where there are houses and a temperate climate is no great problem, but if your locale is tropical and very humid, and if there are no houses, a field laboratory is best forgotten. Even with four walls tropical heat can make processing nearly impossible and will inevitably destroy film.

The requisites for processing film are the darkness of a changing bag, an adequate supply of clean water (it is nice but not absolutely necessary to have it "running"), and a dust-free room for drying negatives. Minimal equipment would include four film tanks for 120 film or two double-reel tanks for 35 mm, one 32-ounce and two 16-ounce plastic beakers, 2 thermometers (you will break one), and a plastic bottle for storing hypo. Ideally do not keep developer; instead use throw-away formulas so that you minimize the risk of failures causd by age-weakened developer. The cheapest and simplest throw-away developer is made from just two easily obtainable chemicals, metol (Eastman calls it Elon) and sodium sulphite —Eastman's formula D-23. Thirty-two ounces of this solution will develop up to twelve rolls of film if you develop them successively in one session; simply add a minute to the developing time for each roll after the sixth. Because this developer deteriorates rapidly with storage, throw it away when you're through. The chemicals are dry and must be weighed with a scales in ounces or grams. A pound of metol and five pounds of sulphite will develop a year's photography for the average field anthropologist. Hypo salts and hypo mixes come dry, but acetic acid comes wet in a glass (never plastic) bottle. You can carry potassium chrome alum powder to use for a film stop-bath, but there is no substitute for an acetic acid stop bath between developing and fixing prints.

The man in the field can make prints by two methods. Without chemicals he can make printing-out proofs, the familiar red-tinted portrait proofs, that are printed by exposing paper and negative in a print frame to the light of the sun; these are only proofs and turn black fairly quickly if exposed to strong daylight. Obviously these are not fit feedback material. The second method is to print your negatives on regular contact paper which requires developing; this necessitates a darkroom, and a "safe-light," a filter of a specified color over a light so you can see well enough to put negative and paper securely into the print frame before you turn on your exposing light. Translated to a darkroom without electricity, this means a safe-light filter secured over a hole in the wall. Printing by daylight calls for a slow contact paper; simply open the door of your darkroom, and close it again quickly. With testing and practice you can print your negatives quite professionally. Ideally you should use an 8- by 10-in. print frame so you can proof or print a complete roll of film at one time. Added equipment for contact print developing would then be a filter to make a safe-light, a print frame, three 8- by 10-in. developing trays, contact paper, dry powder prepared mixes of paper developing chemicals, a bottle of acetic acid, more dry hypo mix, and plastic bottles so you can store your hypo solution and paper developer stock solution. With routine and practice it is possible to process thousands of negatives and efficiently contact print all your material. I had such a darkroom in the Andes and processed six thousand negatives, with the aid of a local helper who quickly learned to develop high quality professional negatives.

The Photographic File

Though gathering data with photography is in many ways a means of simplifying your field effort, it is also in reality an exhaustive chain of effort, beginning with the first-hand observation and ending months or years later in a systematically organized file. Direct observation without the camera, can be at least partially retained in the mind regardless of the loss of notes, but memory process in photography is retained in negatives alone. Should this data stray, become buried under other material, destroyed by vermin or carelessness, the memory storage is lost for good. Hence the care of negatives, contact prints, and identifying data is critical. Filing negatives becomes the final technical link between field observation and research conclusion. A failure in this final process could destroy much of your nonverbal research experience.

Negatives are extremely perishable. They have always been—glass plates that could shatter or nitrate film that could explode and deteriorate by improper storage. All the priceless film footage shot by Kroeber of Ishi, the last "wild" California Indian, was lost, to be found two decades later stored over the steam pipes of the University of California Anthropological Museum. When the can was opened there was nothing left but flakes of nitrate film. Modern negatives are tougher. Safety film will not flash. But negatives can be rendered useless through abrasion and mold.

The greatest threat, however, is outright loss. Negatives have a way of disappearing unless they are stored with maximum security and filed systematically. The great Farm Security Administration file kept a control record of every negative. Every time it was handled, the operation was noted in the laboratory control book. Negatives are so perishable and so easily misplaced that there are agencies in New York City that exist solely to act as custodians of photographers' negative files.

Methods that can insure maximum use of your camera observations literally begin when you make the exposure. Whenever possible keep an adequate film log that can later give on-the-spot insights and reasonable identity for each camera record. As time and distance clouds the memory this log will become increasingly important; indeed, it is the key to the integrity of your records. If you are too harassed to make this record on location, write up this log each night whenever possible.

The second step comes immediately after you have developed your negatives or had them processed. Each negative or frame should be given a chronological number so that the precise order of observation, roll for roll, exposure for exposure, can be irrefutably retained. Professionally film is numbered as it is cut up and stored in glassine envelopes. This should be done before contact printing so that each print will have the negative number on it. Today all 35 mm film is frame numbered so that sequence within the roll is established. This means you can assign a single number to a whole strip of miniature film, and the individual frame is identified by this number plus the edge-number. Some 120 film is also edge numbered, and this number may be incorporated in your system, but your distinguishing number should appear on each frame since negatives of this size are frequently cut up and printed alone. Negatives must be numbered with waterproof ink with a crow-quill drafting pen. Nothing else will hold on the slippery celluloid surface. Roll film should be cut in strips and placed immediately in glassine envelopes. This is done for a number of reasons. It is a hazard to store film rolled up in casarette tins; stored this way it curls like a spring, and makes printing extremely difficult. Film should be stored flat, so that it can be handled without fingering and scratching. Also 35 mm film in cans cannot be examined easily, while cut-up film can be inspected safely through the glassine envelopes. Ideally 35 mm film should be cut in 6-frame strips, 120 in 4-frame strips, 2¼ by 3¼ in. in 3-frame strips, so that they may all be printed roll-for-roll on one sheet of 8- by 10-in. paper. Four sheets of 4- by 10-in. film fits the same size. Thus, a print file from these various negative sizes can be filed uniformly on cards or sheets. Later you may want to select individual negatives for special use in which case negatives 2¼ by 2¼ in. or larger may be cut from their strips and placed in small envelopes; this is more convenient and there is less risk in enlarging. But 35 mm strips should never be cut into individual frames.

Amateurs usually get back their contact prints in single frames. This can be more efficient for single print inspection, but there is a real advantage to having negatives strip-printed in their authentic order. The latter method allows you to see your field studies in organized blocks which is uaually the way you should consider your photographic data. Cutting up your contact sheets exposes photo-records to premature editing and even misplacement of some valuable frame that might become lost to study. We do not, and realistically should not, know what scrap of evidence may form a significant link later, maybe years later in our research. This is why you should resist the temptation of cutting up your contact sheets, lest you lose a genuine control circumstance, that lies in the undistributed relationship of the sequential camera observation. For the times when it *is* methodologically important to work with each frame separately, *make a duplicate set* instead of dismembering your contact sheets.

The most critical step in insuring dynamic research opportunity for your records is the photographic print file. One challenge of a file is to facilitate efficient tracking of selected visual criteria through all of the photographic record. An average file covering a year's work might contain from two to six thousand separate observations, and unless all these views are available to rapid examination, carrying out research within a photographic file becomes time defeating.

Until quite recently this was an equal challenge for the raw data file of interview notes. Even if a file was duplicated a mere five times for cross referencing, raw data covering a few year's field work might fill a large store room. Such an effort would be prohibitively costly. Fortunately modern business methods came to the rescue of the cumbersome cross-reference file with the development of the McBee punch card filing system. File cards of various sizes are manufactured with separate categories represented on each card by a border of numbered holes. This allows for an almost unlimited pattern of cross referencing by clipping out the border of selected categorical numbers. Selection of a reference is accomplished by running a needle through the master card so that all the cards holding the reference you are seeking automatically drop out. This method is being used in many raw data files and is ideally suited for cross-selecting the imagery of photography, as contact prints or groups of prints can be mounted directly on the McBee punch cards.

Of course, there are variations to this ultra efficient system. With the smaller file, or one that is to be used in a general multi-purpose way, single frames can be mounted on a 5-by-7 card which gives ample room for typing in all the identifying data. These cards can then be filed by some basic system of topical divisions with as many subdivisions as might be needed: farming, fishing, lumbering, millwork, fiestas. This variety of file offers special study opportunities. File cards can be removed for select study or shuffled into comparative categories.

Even though a considerable amount of direct research can take place on contact prints, there are many cases of complex process and detail where enlargements clarify and extend the research opportunity. A selected file of 8-by-10-in. *mounted* enlargements of representative material from the master file can function as a key that greatly extends our ability to read detail reliably from small contact prints.

Photographic prints should be mounted or they will curl and crack. A mounted print is infinitely easier to study. The time and expense of mounting is repaid by an efficient use of the file. Mount prints with *dry mounting tissue.* Rubber cement contains sulpher and will stain photographic material in a short time. Dry mounting, even with a household iron, is faster and considerably more permanent.

An important caution: Whenever possible store negatives in a different location from your print files—even in a separate building—so that in the case of fire you will be left with one or the other. Fire or water can destroy a photographic file in minutes.

I conclude this technical writing at the far end of the photographic process with a word of warning—the most deadly end to all our efforts is the photographic file that sits unused. Every attempt should be made to defeat this eventuality by interrelating our file in as many ways as possible with our project's verbal data. Consider that knowledge in our scientific culture is basically verbal, or at least is communicated verbally. Words are more abstract than pictures, and by their simplification more precise. Much of the photographic view is open-ended, challenging you on each inspection to reaffirm opinion. Our filing problem is to tie photography's open door to reality to the verbal abstractions of written data, whether these be the observations of the fieldworker or the words of the native. The real function of the photographic file is to keep alive the cultural moment so that we can consider written field notes with a full sense of the imagery of real circumstances and use the right visual references to vitalize the meaning of the written words.

10

Film for Anthropological Research

THE ENGLISH PHOTOGRAPHER, Muybridge, demonstrating the research use of still photographs taken at controlled intervals, unquestionably laid the basis for the research use of film.[1] His assignment in the 1870s was to settle a bet for Leland Stanford, railroad millionaire and Governor of California, that at a gallop all four of a horse's hooves were off the ground at the same time. This brought about the first scientific recognition that the fleeting details of motion are not stopped by the eye. In 1877 a French astronomer, Jensen, made on one plate a multiple record of the transit of Venus by using a circular daguerreotype plate he turned by hand. Stimulated by both Muybridge and Jensen, the French physiologist and student of movement, Marey, perfected the first moving picture camera—not for entertainment, but strictly to study more than the eye could see.

The modern camera is closely related to this first invention which recorded an image ten or twelve times every second on a continuous spool of sensitized paper. Marey made high speed studies of the flight of pigeons and the running of a horse, which were reported on in his book *Le Mouvement* in 1894. (Michaelis, 1955) In the three-quarters of a century since its development, the moving picture camera has been used extensively for scientific research from astronomy to zoology. In industry, film is the standard method for analyzing the technology of motion for efforts toward efficiency and industrial safety. For related reasons, sports strategists have used film extensively for play-by-play analysis. Psychologists have used film in a similar way in the study of animal and human behavior. In all of these fields it is the flow of film that is so desirable for time and motion analysis.

In anthropology, again it is Margaret Mead and Gregory Bateson who have, together and independently, made the most effective use of film for analysis of cultural behavior (Bateson and Mead, 1942; Mead and Macgregor, 1953). Like Gesell's work in child development (1932; 1945) their work depends not only on the viewing of the film footage, but also on detailed examination and comparison of enlarged prints of single frames.

---

[1] Throughout this chapter "film" means movies.

Yet, in general, film has played only a minor part in anthropological research. This is due in part, I feel, to the fact that film is even harder to harness as data than still pictures. But it is also due to the temptation, or even the pressure, to make films in the field of anthropology for reasons other than research. Great "documentary" films have been made in the field of anthropology by art film makers, and by expert anthropologists. These have generally been produced for an audience, for aesthetic experience, and for education. Film as an *illustration* of culture is unmatched in its ethnographic conviction. Anthropological films as teaching aids represent some of the finest resources in the anthropological library. Many of the best of these efforts are already historical: Flaherty's *Nanook of the North* (1925) and *Man of Aran* (1934), the early document *Grass* by Schoedsack and Cooper (1923), the Canadian Film Board's Indian myth *The Loon's Necklace* (1949).

In recent years anthropologists have turned to film making, producing epics like *The Hunters* by John Marshall and Robert Gardner (1956), Robert Gardner's *Dead Birds* (1964), and vignettes from the culture of Nepal filmed by John and Patricia Hitchcock. Stored in cans are undoubtedly many more yet unedited illustrative documents that would greatly enrich the teaching of anthropology. Also foreign films by their subject and treatment often become useful for teaching anthropology —as for example Satyajit Ray's *Apu Trilogy.*

Because film is so popular a form of entertainment there is always an artistic and commercial temptation to distort the data to conform to more popular taste. The clinical psychologist is not so tempted to strive for artistic effect as is the student of cultures. The clinical observer has more defined reasons for filming whereas popular commercializations have long since invaded the scene of African villages and established concepts of how an audience film on exotic life should look. So in a subtle sense when the anthropologist worries about this audience he may be departing from his goals of scientific recording.

Can these provocative film documents be used for research? Or is there a confusion of ends, in the shooting and the cutting, that makes their use as data difficult or even impossible? There are spontaneous practices that have become conventions in the audience film that are at cross purposes with film data: graphic effects, editorialism in developing the story line, actions out of context, fluency of drawing, and openings and closures so important to story telling.

We have an extreme example in the document *Man of Aran,* unquestionably a great ethnic film. Flaherty's consuming effort was to express his personal vision about the mystique of the Aran Islanders. The film had to have a theme. Flaherty, with intuitive recognition, seized upon two: the struggle to create soil for crops, and the daring in harvesting an economy from the sea. Flaherty then proceeded to document a way of life that had in reality ceased to exist. His film was shot two generations after the fact, a rich and poetic reconstruction of the ethos of the Aran Islanders. It was Flaherty who supplied the authenticity, not the real environment.

The anthropological film maker must face a similar dilemma of ends—gathering controlled comprehensive recordings, or creating provocative film dramas about culture. The challenge lies in deciding how both ends can be met? How can the anthropologist make footage he can use for research, while at the same time gathering educational material for his student audiences?

The Challenge of Scientific Methodology in Film-Making

Anthony R. Michaelis, in his invaluable handbook *Research Films,* presents the richness as well as the intense discipline that has been devoted to film in the biological sciences, including medicine and clinical psychology, where there is little debate about the value of film.

> Cinematography . . . allowed the repeated evaluation of the single experiment; it recorded permanently the most complex patterns of behavior, which it would have been difficult, if not impossible, to describe in verbal terms; and on occasion it has been employed to slow down or to speed up the appearance of the experimental situation (1955:149).

But in the human behavioral sciences the use of film is still in its developing phase. Michaelis brilliantly sums up the oppositional problem.

> A major use of scientific cinematography in anthropology, psychology, and psychiatry is the recording of data under conditions of observation, as distinct from experimentation. In order to make fullest use of such human research and record films it is essential for the scientists to be fully conversant with the sources of error and limitations in the making of these films and also with the conventions developed around the human figure by the commercial cinema; this is particularly so under the less rigidly controlled conditions of field work (1955:167).

Of all the behavioral sciences anthropology is probably the least experimental. The fieldworker in culture must work often in a highly uncontrolled and shifting environment. Michaelis emphasized that even under these uncontrolled circumstances "the research and record film is an invaluable aid as an instrument of observation and description and as a permanent source of data that can be analyzed at leisure." (1955:167) Film then becomes a means of mastering the culturally spontaneous observation by shifting the clinical analysis to the research laboratory where it can be studied *at leisure* and *by any number of specialists.*

It would be enlightening to examine the problems of control and objective authenticity from the moment we choose to photograph to the final editing, observing each phase of film-making as it might add to or subtract from the film's value to research. In film-making, as in shooting still camera records, there is the constant challenge to achieve objectivity or research fidelity. I agree with Michaelis that:

> The moment the photographer sets up a camera in the laboratory or in the field, selects a scene in the viewfinder, and presses the starter button, his whole personality has been brought into play, and a theoretically objective technique has changed into a subjective statement (1955:167).

This covers the whole field of anthropological photography and, again, introduces the problem of scientific control to cope with this ever present challenge of objectivity.

As with still camera recording, the first scientific decision is to choose the significant target areas which when covered will offer a structured view of your research. This does not mean an inhibiting preselection of data; it simply means to control the roving camera sufficiently so creative spontaneous shooting *within* a sample of study points will contain the evidence necessary for a conclusive statment.

After the point of no return, when we face our data in the laboratory, there always develops a bare-bones model of just the evidence we *must* have to conclude our study objectively. The anticipation of these needs should be, whenever possible, the basis of sampling in the field.

Each target area of the research contains this methodological challenge. Most fieldworkers do not have two cameras to allow for hours of uninterrupted shooting. The average camera run is 30 seconds, and a 100 feet of film runs out in 2 minutes at 24 frames per second. There *must* be breaks regardless of how extravagant our film supply is. Every time we push the starter button we are sampling elements within the immediate filming circumstances. For many circumstantial reasons, sometimes a hundred feet of film must be made to cover the episode. What should our criteria be for selecting and budgeting our film?

A workman-like understanding could be arrived at by forgetting about research needs and simply considering the problem of practical documentation, when the whole record of an event is the objective. Alexander H. Leighton tells of an experience with an Eskimo on St. Lawrence Island that gives an example of thoroughly functional film selectivity. A teacher on the island (a white man) asked an Eskimo friend to take some shots of a whale hunt with the white man's amateur movie camera. Leighton saw the results and was so impressed with the film that he looked up the Eskimo, curious as to where the man had learned film-making. When Leighton asked, the embarrassed Eskimo told him, "That's the only film I ever made!"

Realistically, it was probably the Eskimo's sense of the importance of technology as a part of survival that had prompted him to look-up directions in the instruction book for the camera, which he had seen lying by the teacher's desk. Armed with this information he had proceeded to film a complete whale hunt on one roll of film. Leighton remembers that the film was evenly exposed throughout, which means that the Eskimo had grasped the optical principle or exposure and made the necessary adjustments for changes in light. Leighton further recalls that the camera runs were neither too short nor too long, which I take to mean that he shot longer runs on important elements and shorter runs on trivia. Like the weaver in Otavalo (see Chap. 4), the Eskimo was an expert in his subject—hunting whales. His film-making was functionally sound. He *did* have target foresight; he knew what the critical elements of a whale hunt were. This professionalism went into all his filming decisions. His goal was not art, but how to kill a whale. Even with his short load of film he held back a last precious run *in case* they harpooned a whale. Film in the camera was like ammunition in his rifle. Never be caught empty! They *did* harpoon a whale, so that his document was dramatically complete, with the thrashing of the whale's flukes and the swirling of blood in the sea![2]

We cannot be all-in-one experts in hunting, fishing, and weaving, but we can study our processes before filming so that our selectivity is functional, and each filmed unit can be architecturally as complete as possible.

Next in order of filming is where to stand, the questions of camera angles, choice of lenses, or zooms. The multiple lens system is an answer to near and far

---

[2] Private communication.

filming without moving the camera. Usually a revolving turret holds a wide-angle lens, a medium focal length lens, and a telephoto lens, but there must be a film break when the photographer swivels from one lens to the other. The zoom is an all-purpose multi-focal lens that allows the photographer every gradation from a wide angle view to a telephoto view with the same lens. This allows for unbroken sequences of close-up to distance filming. The goal of filming should be to see as clearly as possible what is going on. Priority in decision making should always go to clarity of view. When details are obscure, zoom in or turret to your 90 mm lens. Turret to your extreme wide-angle lens when sweeping relationships of social inter-action or technology are essential to documentary clarity. Plan your shooting so cam-era runs will blanket comprehensive wholes. This will later offer you footage which you can use in research. Monitor your camera load so that you have an unbroken ep-isode when you need it. And budget your total film supply so that your target areas are covered, both for your research and for audience film.

Beyond intelligent filming, research film often needs various control ele-ments that relate the shooting to the passage of time, to the exact identification of where and when each unit was filmed, and devices for reliably interrelating the filming with other research techniques and activities.

Professional film-makers have always used slates to keep scenes in order. In both stills and films this is a basic technique of identification and control; in clinical films clocks are often present. In filming craft processes in the field time relations may be equally essential; a wide-faced clock placed in the crafting scene could pace a documentation and make otherwise chaotic detail an orderly part of the record. If later cutting is essential to fluency, clocking your camera runs would be essential to assembling a research document. In the laboratory, runs of unidentifiable film are like "pieces of string too short to use." They may make artistic filler, but they would mutilate the body of an authentic data film. If you are shooting a sound film, a tape recorder is your best monitor. This will later allow you to preserve the exact se-quence in splicing and cutting. Match the sound and you have complete control of the order of scenes.

Again, as with still recording, keeping a photographic log is an essential aid to authentic order. This may be a two-man job. This is not an extravagance, for film-making often *is* more than a one-man job. It can involve a crew of fieldwork-ers, professional or native. Technological and cultural elements can become so com-plex that they must be taken care of simultaneously to make film documents possi-ble.

The most controversial control factor of all is the final assembling of the raw data film. Should research film be cut? Will this destroy the research authentic-ity? Certainly it is possible to destroy film data by scientifically insensitive cutting, but, on the other hand, there are film-making anthropologists who feel sensible cut-ting can enhance the data film. They feel cutting is no different from selective shooting. "Every time you push or stop pushing the button you cut." This is practi-cally true. The other side of the controversy can also point out that cutting often does destroy the research opportunity and data film should be left just as it was shot! This instinctive caution is well founded; after all you do not edit your field notebooks. Possibly the problem of researching from raw data film might suggest that intelligent cutting could make this job a lot easier, at least for other people. Consider the practical problem. There are strictly optical happenings in filming having nothing to do with the data. Every time you push the button on a Bell and Howell you get an empty frame; certainly these should be cut out simply to save your eyes while studying the film. There are apt to be hosts of optical failures that should also be cut out. Then there is the problem of spontaneous shooting during the filming episode. The creative photographer responds to spontaneous happenings that are neither central to the research event, nor have proper time place when the events are recorded; it may be wise to remove them, or functional to cut them into the data where they intelligently fit. Your sensitivity tells you when to shoot, and the same sensitivity tells you when to edit. It would be very limiting to inhibit this kind of selectivity. If there is a rule of thumb, let it be: Never cut data film unless there is a very functional reason to do so, and never cut so as to deface the basic temporal pattern of your evidence.

We can constructively apply to this problem the requirements of making still photographs that can be computed. It is clear that in order to read out the data it must be photographed into the records by selectivity, sampling, and adequate repetition so fluent interpretations can later be made.

If this selectivity does not take place, computing film can become so complicated as to defeat the ends of the research on an extensive film document. As an illustration, consider the problem Paul Ekman had to overcome in analyzing only a short sample of film in his Nonverbal Research Center at Langley Porter Clinic in San Francisco. Here the subjects were filmed against a grid during a structured interview so that all body motions could be related to the interview content. To research his film took twenty-four hours of study for one minute of film by the aid of the PerceptoScope.[3]

Compare this clinically controlled circumstance with a puberty rite in Africa and you can appreciate how exhausting the problem of using film as data can be. Or examine the challenge when anthropologists do attempt the comprehensive film document. In Samuel A. Barrett's effort to salvage passing cultures on film, his crew recorded in 1963 four major Navajo ceremonies: the Red Ant Way, a girl's puberty ceremony, the Mountain Chant, and a Yebitchai. Three of these ceremonies were recorded in their complete nine-day form. A report on this project states, "While none of the Navajo material has been released in the form of educational films, the total footage, 46,000 feet, represents the most complete record of these ceremonies" (Peri and Wharton 1965:34). Indeed it would be a staggering accomplishment to compute all the data available in this 46,000 feet of ceremonial film.

The point is the flow of film through the movie camera records such masses of imagery, that the selecting out of the responsibly readable variables becomes extremely difficult. Recently an art film maker produced an epic record of a man sleeping for eight hours. Possibly this controlled effort *could* be totally computed!

---

[3] The PerceptoScope is a hand-held electrical control that allows the viewer complete control over the movement of the film, forward runs, backward runs, repeats, and stops for detailed frame-for-frame inspection. Film simply cannot be thoroughly computed without such a tool.

The Challenge of the Budget

The very practical problem of budget certainly has discouraged research films. On the commercial market films cost not less than $1000 a minute. Estimates for a thirty-minute educational ethnographic film range from $15,000 minimum for a professionally-made black-and-white unsynchronized sound film, to $5000 for a film shot by the fieldworker with relatively little cutting and minimal use of laboratory refinements such as fades and dissolves. John and Patricia Hitchcock present a detailed review of the economic variables that go into ethnographic film-making in their article in the *American Anthropologist* (1960). My own experimental film described below—a forty-five minute black-and-white silent film with no laboratory opticals, titling, or technical refinements—cost less than $500, a budget that covers just the cost of film, developing, and printing. But even this figure is costly for many anthropologists' photographic budget when you must add to it the cost of movie equipment.

Can the average anthropological field budget afford research with film that must also be used for audience education? Is cinematography at this level possible only with lush grants? Foundations providing more than $10,000 for a film are likely to expect a professional fulfillment which means budgeting for an experienced camera man. Unquestionably film-making is a most expensive item, and too often it carries a commitment of producing a popular film to offset the prohibitive field expense. It is here that the trails of research and audience film often part, and the anthropologist returns with a travelog instead of film cans of data.

If film is so expensive, and it certainly is time consuming, why not use a still camera instead of a movie camera? Certainly this question should be answered before you invest in a $400 camera and several hundred dollars' worth of film. The still camera *cannot* do what the movie camera can do, whereas the movie camera can approximate everything the still camera can record. This means that the unwary anthropologist often uses his 16 mm movie camera at seven dollars every two minutes, as if it were a still camera, in situations where the Leica could do the same recording for 22 cents' worth of bulk load film. This may be expedient in an educational film, but it is an absurd extravagance in gathering photographic data.

Can anthropologists do significant recording with film for less than a thousand dollars? And can such a low budget avoid the technical comprises that would make it impossible to use a film for audience as well as research? If you are filming for raw data alone, cycles of research activities could be filmed adequately with $100 worth of film. Using a 16 mm camera this would yield 25 minutes of data. On 8 mm you would get 100 minutes of research film.

The challenge is to bring back reasonable educational footage as well as research sequences. How small a budget could you have and still make this possible? Before we examine this question it would help to look at some of the needs of an educational film that would have to be considered along with our research needs in the film circumstance. A well-taken research film might never make a persuasive educational document; such footage could be lacking in the linkage between scenes essential for a flowing story-telling film.

Just as textbooks are improved with literary merit, an educational film must also be sufficiently complete and flowing so that complex aspects of culture can be grasped by the student audience. In field conditions during film-making this suggests the need for structure in designing, timing, interlocking, and a comprehensive completion so that conceptual insights can be formed by the projected film.

This *could* collide disastrously with documentary research aims, but if you are able to weave these needs into your frame of reference this collision of interests does not have to take place. The structural conceptions necessary for your audience film could be considered simply as a more refined order of field observation if your film goal *is* this comprehensive view.

Circumstances Where Film Recording Is Invaluable

If audience film is not the goal, the movie camera would be a specialized tool used for gathering particular data that could be recorded in no other way. It is film's unbroken record that offers its distinctive research possibility and at the same time makes it prohibitively expensive. Therefore, if we do use film for research, we must recognize in advance the varieties of recordings that can be the subject of direct research analysis. As in still photography, some areas of documentation are more stably understood than others. One way to recognize these areas is to be clear about what observations can only be reliably made by film. This would allow us to simplify reading as well as outlining distinct areas where we could conceivably do research in anthropology with film.

Even though the movie camera *can* approximate still camera recordings, like samples of houses on the village street, analyzing data from projected movie film is exhausting. For one thing we do not have the opportunity for multiple examination of enlarged photographs for precise comparison. Film cannot be handed around and talked about like photographs, or looked at with a fine glass. We can stop the projector to examine the single frame but we cannot compare this frame directly with another except by printed enlargements made from the single frames. So when material is to be computed, record with the still camera whenever it will do the job. Where particularly saturated coverage is needed the robot camera with automatic time-sampling controls, may be a mid-point between stills and movies.

The movie camera's value in recording technology and ceremony has been refined for us by films used in industry and engineering. Film is *the* tool for analysis of process where technological innovation or subtle abstraction on technological change is needed. In anthropology film is not only the complete way of recording choreography, but also the most direct way of analyzing dance or ceremony, where so many elements are in motion together. In this situation human memory and note-book recordings become wholly inadequate and highly impressionistic. Traffic engineers face the same problem in analyzing highway bottle necks. It is the net effect of thousands of drivers that must be observed in *motion*. Film can become the safety engineer's vital data.

These applications lay down some guide lines for a practical research use of the ethnographer's movie camera. When you shoot do so with unbroken fluency, plan your filming from one scene to another. Do not stop in the middle of significant action, even if this means the use of two cameras. Research unit-to-unit value lies in its continuity. The research possibilities of film drop off in direct ratio to the fractured character of the shooting. A snip here and there of cultural sequence has little value to film research.

Only the moving picture film can record the realism of time and motion, or the psychological reality of varieties of interpersonal relations. As an example, it is hard to evaluate the character of love between children and parents from still photographs, whereas film can record the family tempo, the nature of touching, how long, how often, and the way an older sister expresses fondness for a younger brother. The emotional chain is too broken in still photographs; its time slices are too far apart unless we have a camera that mechanically exposes a frame every five seconds, and even then the emotional tempo would be confused.

Communication in Three Families, by Gregory Bateson, illustrates the humanistic research value of the film. This observational training film for psychiatrists, is an unbroken record of two-circumstances—giving the baby his bath and feeding the baby—in three families. Bateson selected these two episodes for saturated filming because he felt psychiatric students should be able to responsibly read the personality and psychological matrix established within families by so many processes besides the spoken word. Two movie cameras were used by two camera men, Bateson and his assistant, in order to keep an unbroken log. Each time the camera ran out of film, the time break was indicated by cutting in the image of the next photographer. The importance of this experiment was that certain psychological aspects could be examined in the same way by any number of observers, so these aspects could be pointed out and the recognition transferred to interpretation of other psychiatric evaluations.

The circumstances suggested in the outline below are areas where the field-worker studying family culture in this country might shoot short but comprehensive sequences, scenes having fluent readable data, and, where an audience film was a commitment. Research scenes might be woven into a lengthy educational document, so that there would be both a research return and a story-telling film. Of course in another culture the circumstances and emotions attending similar function would be quite different.

Shooting Script for a Day with an American Family

A sleeping child wakes and responds to his immediate circumstances of well-being, of love or loneliness, of the familiar or unfamiliar.

Attention paid to children in the rush to get the day started, older children to school, father to his job.

Interpersonal contact during the rushed morning meal.

Proximity and emotional interchange between young children playing: tender, considerate, generous, rough, aggressive, cruel, emotionally together or very isolated—or perhaps all these.

Noontime meal: is it a social game? Or is it just to cram away food?

Mother at work: interacts with children emotionally, or ignores them, pushes them aside.

Father at work: how he uses his tools: skillfully, with form and self expression, lays them down with care? *Or* shows little skill, uses tools injuriously, drops them without affection or respect?

Father joins a social gathering for lunch with other workers: he is greeted jovially, other men show respect and signal his popularity, men listen when he talks; *or* crowd ignores him, greetings casual, they do not listen when he speaks.

Children respond to father when he returns from work: ignore him, cling to him; does he accept or reject their affections?

Children are a part of the adult meal, parents listen to children, respond; *or* children ignored, pushed aside, father only wants to talk to mother.

Time for bed. Is going to bed an affectionate game? How relaxed and happy are the children? How do they drift off to sleep: clutching each other, or relaxed? Twist and turn in bed, appear tense or resentful?

Each one of these suggested film scenes contains a complete unit of emotional and physical reality to be read and interpreted by any number of analysts. The key to the data is found in the fluency of motion by which so many attitudes of emotion and value are expressed. These behavior phenomena are often not clear in still photographs. Family studies with the still camera suggest this variety of experience, but these records remain impressionistic since the continuity of the experience is fractured. As Birdwhistell says, "One of the unexpected rewards of multiple re-examination of film is that many students for the first time get the idea that 'natives' are human" (1963:58). In effect, the value of film is that it is alive and warm, while in a popular way still photographs are dead; from a purely scientific point of view this is also true.

An Experimental Film Record: *A Family's Day*

Can valid data footage be made into an audience film, and through an authentic continuity of record preserve scientific integrity? To test this possibility I made an experimental field film along the lines suggested above.

In conducting this experiment I had two major goals: to make as much film as possible with a budget of $400 in a simulated field circumstance, and to shoot the film so there would be a maximum of undisturbed data creating an intelligible audience film. To attain these goals meant an experiment in preselection and arrangement that would require minimal cutting in the final production.

I also kept in mind the concrete field problem so methodologically the experiment would be of practical application to field anthropology. With this approach I decided to make as whole a view as possible of a family. This might be ideally filmed toward the end of an extended field study when rapport was strongest and our ethnographic knowledge adequate.

Even under ideal circumstances film requires far more control and rapport than still photography. Making film cannot be compared to the still camera's unobtrusive function, when used for orientation in the first weeks of a field expedition. Film-making, by the nature of its uninterrupted flow, is a formal procedure that requires the understanding and cooperation of a community or a family. A prestudy with the still camera could be considered an excellent introduction to filming, both in educating the actors and in researching the filming possibilities. The experimental film I am going to describe was made with this background. I was on intimate terms with the subjects. All of the family had been extensively photographed, and had been gratified with the feedback of their own images. You might say I made use of a year of my field time to achieve a relationship of this character. In fact, the whole native community had become used to my recording with cameras at social gatherings—along with good food, wine, and music.

In my simulated field situation, I had with me just 2000 feet of black-and-white 16 mm film, partly fast Tri-X and partly slow Panchromatic film. I was equipped with a Bell and Howell D. H. with three lenses (a wide angle, a medium, and a telephoto), a good movie tripod with a pan head, and a light meter. To add more scientific value I asked a collaborator to pace each scene with the Leica so that we would have both stills and film for laboratory study.

Our first task was what to sample in our native family's day: (1) What actually was going on during the filming period of two days; and (2) What the family agreed was important to present a cycle of their life. These decisions suggested only a few arranged scenes, the most important being a social gathering which had to be organized and required the second day of shooting. To have a comprehensive view it was necessary to go backward in time to pick up circumstances the family agreed were important. For example, because college was over for the summer we reviewed the routine of studying for college as our native showed us authentically where and how he studied. This pulling together of time elements can be culturally undistorting if the native directs his own role. This is a form of "socio-drama-interviewing."

The film was directed most of the time by this "acting out" technique. Our family was asked to do everything with just the same pace as they would always carry out their chores. This intent was explained clearly to the family's children, and after a few periods of tension, the family was able to relax and interact spontaneously before the camera.

During the filming I constantly kept in mind long runs, and runs between actions, so that events could flow without over-cutting the film. Our whole expedition's supply of film ran through the camera in two days. While I was exposing 2000 feet of film worth $150, my partner was covering the same events with four rolls of bulk-wound 35 mm film worth $.80. It should be evident that every minute of film was irreplaceable! Shooting as openly as I did for both research and smooth film meant we had just one opportunity to make this document. Hence in the field circumstance we were gambling our whole film budget on one occasion; we would have no film for retakes. So we had to have control, structure, and an image of data in mind before we began to shoot. But the things that happened within our selective phases of the family day were spontaneous and uncontrived cultural phenomena. The scenes were positive samples of undisturbed reality preserving and offering genuine research opportunities.

I shot 16 mm negative film. Ideally I urge you to use reversal film, as most television producers do, for it makes cutting your master film easier. We bought the best print we could order, a timed print that would be suitable for audience viewing. This print was cut to remove light fog from loading and a few camera failures. Rolls were simply spliced together in their proper order. The finished print was cut by about one-fifth to just under 1600 feet, about 45 minutes of film projected at 24 frames per second.

Our film was silent, but the circumstances of the film were rich with aural data. We decided to attempt to gather simultaneously at least some of this material. During the social gathering we taped conversation and singing, and for the closing we recorded putting the children to bed—a small investment of one roll of tape.

When the film was complete we borrowed a second tape-recorder and made a tape from selected parts of the master tape to go with the scenes of the social gathering and the children going to bed. This left 60 percent of the film silent. As this appeared disturbing, we filled in with guitar music that the family was fond of, plus overlaps of their own music. This was a concession to our audience, and in no way distorted the valid film content.

An anti-climax to the whole experiment was that the film was badly scratched by a faulty projector and we had to have a second print made! This meant cutting the untouched master negative. Friends told me this might take a week of tedious work visually matching the negative to our cut positive, for we had not had our negative edge-numbered. Actually I cut some 1900 feet of film in 6 hours; for there was no cutting within the scenes. I matched rolls, cut out fog and technical failures, and spliced in series. This was a forceful demonstration of how little cutting actually went into this 40-minute educational film.

Final Figures for A Family's Day

The shooting stock, 16 mm neg.	$150
Development of neg. @ 2¢ a foot	40
Print @ 5¢ a foot	100
Recording tape	4
Second print, 1600 ft. @ 5¢	80
Miscellaneous	26
	$400

Was there genuine research value in this footage? Two controlled tests were run—one in the Anthropology Department at Stanford University, and one at San Francisco State College—to weigh just what had been recovered by the film. To deepen this evaluation, the Leica stills of each scene were enlarged and exhibited for group study. Students wrote down as much data as they could observe from the stills. This gave rounded ethnographic insight of kinds of property, kinds of technology, costumes, and material values of the home. After this analysis the film was screened, and in both experiments the students were able to extend their observations. In particular the students felt that the qualities of love, qualities of child-to-child and child-to-parent relationships, which were only implied in the stills, were clearly definable in the film. Nor could the stills tell anything about the tempo of the family's life.

Quite reasonably the film did offer these insights. This further supports our view of what film can offer anthropology—the emotional character of culture and the psychological content of human relationships.

A Different Experimental Film: *The Sucking Doctor*

What might be the best possible research and audience film assuming the anthropologist had $5000 to make a documentary? Would the basic problem change from the minimal budget film? The methodological challenge remains the same, to carry out an extremely demanding variety of observations within spontaneous cultural situations. If the filming effort is over-controlled and structured, we may have a film that projects the producer's image but fails to record an authentic happening. In one sense, the more impressive the operation the further refined the research control has to be.

An experiment in the ultimate film research document developed out of Samuel A. Barrett's monolithic ethnographic film project sponsored by the National Science Research Council. Dr. Barrett's studies were not directed toward anthropological research with film, but were museological views of the last remnants of California, Northwest Coast, Plains, and Southwest Indian crafts and ceremonies. The goal was to partially reconstruct sequences of the way Indian culture might have been before the days of massive cultural intrusion. Dr. Barrett's effort resulted in a brilliant salvage record.

Members of Barrett's staff, cinema photographer William Heick and anthropologists Robert Wharton and David Peri, were interested in carrying the research beyond Dr. Barrett's shorter documents into an embracing documentary that would offer open-ended research into all parts of a modern Indian ceremonial.[4] Their approach sought for the contemporary Indian image in speech, habitat, clothing, and technology rather than a scholarly reproduction of classical culture that is perishing.

Independently, with their own funds, they made an extreme effort at whole, uninterrupted documentation of a Pomo curing ceremony, in a two hour film cycle called *The Sucking Doctor*. This film was the result of four years of planning and human relations within the Stewart's Point Pomo Indian community. Peri himself is part Pomo, a distant relative of a matriarchal religious leader and Indian revivalist, who was a central figure in the Stewart's Point community. In this Indian community they had filmed for Dr. Barrett various short studies, preparing acorn meal, weaving baskets, and so on, and Peri had repeatedly asked his relative for permission to film a healing ceremony. Finally the woman shaman consented, a date was set.

Technology of the Filming and Methodological Control

Two elements were a necessity if this was to be a research film: (1) the complete ceremony must be filmed with uninterrupted sound and motion; (2) there must be controls that would allow the data to be held in authentic position for re-

---

[4] This report is based on conversations with Heick, Peri, and Wharton.

search analysis. The finest equipment was rented, a Nagra tape-recorder, an Auricon sound camera that recorded on tape as well as film, an Arriflex to be used as a "wild" camera that shot silently, and a Bell and Howell 100-foot load camera. The Auricon had a 1200-foot magazine with a 33-minute run, and the Arriflex a 400-foot magazine with a 12-minute run. Each camera had a zoom and a wide-angle lens. The Nagra tape-recorder was used as the major control of all sequence; it was wired to the Auricon so the film track had a synchronized signal that could be matched exactly with the sound flow of recorder. In turn, the continuous filming of the Auricon acted as a control over the Arriflex by optical comparison. Beyond these technologies, a minute-by-minute film log was made as well as an anthropological log, so that events not covered by the cameras could be related to the exact footage of film. Photographically, the Auricon was on a heavy tripod in a *fixed* position. Its only movements were modest panning, zooming in for close-ups and turreting to the wide-angle lens for a complete view. As the healing took place within a prescribed area which the film-makers could not enter, close-ups were filmed entirely with the zoom.

The Arriflex, which could be used on or off the tripod, had two functions: as a standby camera when the Auricon magazines were being changed; and as a roving camera which attempted to cover actions unobservable from the fixed position of the Auricon. Footage principally from the Arriflex and to a limited extent from the Bell and Howell was *cut into* the Auricon film in the final editing whenever it was filling in for the Auricon, or when it had supplementary footage that was important to the record. The team wanted this effort to be for both audience and research, so when the footage of the stationary Auricon became visually monotonous, the other material was cut in to give the document film sense. *This cutting in was in accurate time relationship.* No live action was spliced in out of controlled sequence; a limited amount of static material unrelated to the action was spliced cut of sequence to enhance the document for audience viewing. The master sound track of the Nagra tape-recorder was left complete and undisturbed on the final edited print.

Under William Heick's direction the dance house where the ceremony was to take place was prepared. There was no light in the house but a central wood fire. To keep the artificial light from being a distracting factor one lead wire was buried in the dirt floor and only two lights were hung: a thousand-watt flood up in the smoke hole, and a smaller filler light at one side to give detail in the shadows. Because of the limited light, the document was shot on Tri-X black-and-white film, knowingly one stop underexposed; this was compensated for by forced development in processing.

Though two nights of ceremony were filmed, the team decided they could only afford to present a finished production of one night of undisturbed ceremony, so the final film shows the activities of the second night, which they felt to be the more complete performance. In addition to the actual ceremony a small amount of footage was shot for cut-away material that might be needed in the making of audience film. The total footage shot was 3800 feet for two nights of filming: 2600 feet for the Auricon and 1200 for the Arriflex, a ratio of 2:1 for the Auricon. The flow of the Auricon was cut as little as possible in the final version, with an editing ratio of 5:1 in favor of the Auricon. The final film is 1600 feet, which makes a ratio of approximately 1:1 when only the second night's filming is considered; this is a most unusual accomplishment in film.

Expenses for The Sucking Doctor

Film and processing	*ca.*	$1200
Rental of equipment		150
Lights		40
Recording tape—4 rolls @ $3.50		14
Miscellaneous	*ca.*	20
Fees to participants		200
Final print		278

Estimated total $1902

Thus the total cost of *The Sucking Doctor* falls considerably below the $5000 suggested by the Hitchcocks (1960). But Heick feels the Hitchcocks' figure was accurate for any overseas production. Also, Heick points out that many corners were cut with local economic know-how and technique beyond the skills of the average anthropological film-maker.

In final consideration, the team considered that they had made compromises to the audience film image. Robert Wharton felt it was halfway between an audience production and raw research footage. The question is: what research data might have been dulled or omitted? Conceivably breaking the monotony by cutting out and in from the second camera could have lost sequence evidence. The choice of lighting was a makeshift compromise in favor of dramatic effect. The only natural light was the fire and to make filming easier they used a high floodlight as the main source of light for the ceremony. This was a modest distortion. Heick in afterthought suggested that they might have fed magnesium foil into the wood fire and used *this* for the major light source! Despite these compromises, *The Sucking Doctor* is an outstanding research film and probably the most complete documentary anthropological film made to date.

Conclusion

How is data film for research finally used? The realities of the film computing process are startling, because in effect, most research shifts from the fluid achievement of film, back to the analysis of single frames, in much the same fashion as Muybridge analyzed animal locomotion. Gesell reduced film back to still frames (1945), and most biological film analysis tends to be a process of noting minute change from frame to frame.

Film's great asset to research is its automatic sequence control that allows for the most complete analysis of time slices. The very concept of "continuity" means ordered and unbroken sequence. When the researcher wants to analyze a precise development in continuity, he must be able to control the projector, as with the Percepto-Scope (see footnote 3, Chap. 10). Another device does the same with the added advantage of sound. Ray Birdwhistell (1963:58) and Paul Ekman are among those who depend on such equipment for their research.

But the intensely objective frame-for-frame analysis is only one achievement in photography for anthropology. In both media, still and film, there remains first and last the persuasive realism, that at one time inhibits clinical study and at another offers anthropology its most complete view of culture. The photographic impressionism that makes the scientist wary of camera records, also represents the comprehensiveness of film and still records, that allows us to respond to real experience. As anthropologists let us not lose sight of this brilliance.

Camera records *can* bring into the laboratory all the pitfalls of first hand observation. Let us make the most of this realism, and appreciate that the difficulty of photographic evidence *is* fundamentally the problem of scientific observation by any means—not some special fault of the camera record. If we want to use photography with more research acuity, let us constantly return to the instant of exposure. We may master how to read all details and relations within pictures, but the significant recovery will never be made if the vision that triggered the record is not equally refined. Rich research imagery of culture can only come through enriched sensory perception.

References

BATESON, GREGORY, 1963, "Exchange of Information about Patterns of Human Behavior." In *Information Storage and Neural Control*. William Fields and Walter Abbott (eds.). Springfield, Ill.: Charles C Thomas.

————, and MARGARET MEAD, 1942, *Balinese Character: A Photographic Analysis*. New York: New York Academy of Sciences Special publication.

BIRDWHISTELL, RAY L., 1952, *Introduction to Kinesics*. Louisville, Ky.: University of Louisville Press.

————, 1963, "The Use of Audio-Visual Teaching Aids." In *Resources for the Teaching of Anthropology*. David G. Mandelbaum and others (eds.). Memoir No. 95 of the American Anthropological Association.

BYERS, PAUL, 1964, "Still Photography in the Systematic Recording and Analysis of Behavioral Data." *Human Organization*, Vol. 23, pp. 78–84.

————, 1966, "Cameras Don't Take Pictures." The Columbia University Forum, IX: Vol. 1, pp. 27–31.

CATHEY, ALYCE, 1965, "A Study of Low-Fifth Girl Grouping at Noon: 12:00 Lunch Group and 12:15–12:50 Game Group." Unpublished manuscript.

COLLIER, GEORGE, and EVON Z. VOGT, 1965, "Aerial Photographs and Computers in the Analysis of Zinacanteco Demography and Land Tenure." Paper presented at the 64th Annual Meeting of the American Anthropological Association, Denver. (mimeographed.)

COLLIER, JOHN, JR., 1957, "Photography in Anthropology: A Report on Two Experiments." *American Anthropologist*, Vol. 59, pp. 843–859.

————, and ANIBAL BUITRON, 1949, *The Awakening Valley. Chicago:* The University of Chicago Press.

EGLI, EMIL, 1960, *Europe from the Air*. Hans Richard Müller (ed.). New York: Funk and Wagnalls.

GESELL, ARNOLD, 1945, "Cinemanalysis: A Method of Behavior Study." *Journal of General Psychology*, Vol. 47, p. 3.

————, and others, 1934, *An Atlas of Infant Behavior*. New Haven, Conn.: Yale University Press.

GOLDSCHMIDT, WALTER, and ROBERT B. EDGERTON, 1961, "A Picture Technique for the Study of Values." *American Anthropologist*, Vol. 63, No. 1, pp. 26–47.

HALL, EDWARD T., 1959, *The Silent Language*. New York: Doubleday.

————, 1966, *The Hidden Dimension*. New York: Doubleday.

HEUSCH, LUC DE, 1962, "The Cinema and Social Science: A Survey of Ethnographic and Sociological Films." *Reports and Papers in the Social Science*, No. 16. Paris: UNESCO.

HITCHCOCK, JOHN T., and PATRICIA J. HITCHCOCK, 1960, "Some Considerations for the Prospective Ethnographic Cinematographer." *American Anthropologist*, Vol. 62, pp. 656–674.

HONIGMANN, JOHN JOSEPH, 1954, *Culture and Personality*. New York: Harper & Row.

LEWIS, OSCAR, 1961, *The Children of Sanchez: Autobiography of a Mexican Family*. New York: Random House.

LYNES, RUSSELL, 1957, *The Taste Makers*. New York: Harper & Row.

MEAD, MARGARET, 1963, "Anthropology and the Camera." In *The Encyclopedia of Photography*, Vol. 1, pp. 166–184. Willard D. Morgan (ed.). New York: Greystone Press.

———, and PAUL BYERS, 1967, *The Small Conference*, The Hague: Mouton & Co. N.V.

———, and FRANCES COOKE MACGREGOR, 1951, *Growth and Culture: A Photographic Study of Balinese Childhood*. Based upon photographs by Gregory Bateson, analyzed in Gesell categories. New York: Putnam.

MICHAELIS, ANTHONY R., 1955, *Research Films in Biology, Anthropology, Psychology, and Medicine*. New York: Academic Press.

NEWHALL, BEAUMONT, 1949, *The History of Photography from 1839 to the Present Day*. New York: Museum of Modern Art.

PERI, DAVID W., and ROBERT W. WHARTON, 1965, "Samuel Alfred Barrett: 1879–1965." In *Kroeber Anthropological Society Papers*, Vol. 33, pp. 3–28.

REDFIELD, ROBERT, 1955, *The Little Community: Viewpoints for the Study of a Human Whole*. Chicago: University of Chicago Press.

ROBERTS, JOHN M., 1951, *Three Navajo Households: A Comparative Study of Small Group Culture*. Papers of the Peabody Museum of American Archeology and Ethnology, Vol. 40, No. 3. Cambridge, Mass.: Harvard University Press.

ROTMAN, ARTHUR, 1964, "The Value of Photographic Technique in Plotting Sociometric Interaction." Paper presented at the Annual Meeting of the Southwestern Anthropological Association, San Francisco.

RUESCH, JURGEN, and WELDON KEES, 1956, *Nonverbal Communication: Notes on the Visual Perception of Human Relations*. Berkeley and Los Angeles: University of California Press.

SMITH, W. EUGENE, 1958, "Drama Beneath a City Window: Sixth Avenue Photographs." *Life*, March 10, 1958, Vol. 44, pp. 107–114.

SPINDLER, GEORGE, and LOUISE SPINDLER, 1965, "The Instrumental Activities Inventory: A Technique for the Study of the Psychology of Acculturation." *Southwestern Journal of Anthropology*, Vol. 21, pp. 1–23.

TREMBLAY, MARC-ADÉLARD, JOHN COLLIER, JR., and TOM T. SASAKI, 1954, "Navajo Housing in Transition." *America Indígena*, Vol. 14, No. 3, pp. 187–218.

WARNER, LLOYD, and others, 1949, *Social Class in America: A Manual of Procedure for the Measurement of Social Status*. Chicago: Science Research Associates.

WERNER, OSWALD, 1961, "Ethnographic Photography." Abstract of Thesis, Indiana University. (mimeographed.)

GENERAL EDITORS

GEORGE AND LOUISE SPINDLER
Stanford University

UNDERSTANDING AN AFRICAN KINGDOM: BUNYORO
John Beattie, *Oxford University*

VISUAL ANTHROPOLOGY: PHOTOGRAPHY AS
A RESEARCH METHOD
John Collier, Jr., *San Francisco State College*

ANALYSIS OF PREHISTORIC ECONOMIC PATTERNS
Creighton Gabel, *Boston University*

HOW TO LEARN AN UNWRITTEN LANGUAGE
Sarah C. Gudschinsky, *Summer Institute of Linguistics*

THE LIFE HISTORY IN ANTHROPOLOGICAL SCIENCE
L. L. Langness, *University of Washington*

MANUAL FOR KINSHIP ANALYSIS
Ernest L. Schusky, *Southern Illinois University*

FIELD METHODS IN THE STUDY OF CULTURE
Thomas Rhys Williams, *The Ohio State University*

Related Titles
in
CASE STUDIES IN CULTURAL ANTHROPOLOGY

BUNYORO: AN AFRICAN KINGDOM
John Beattie

THE DUSUN: A NORTH BORNEO SOCIETY
Thomas Rhys Williams

HOLT, RINEHART AND WINSTON, INC.
383 Madison Ave., New York 10017